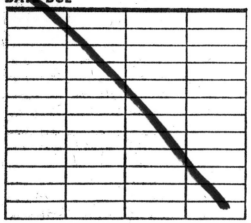

Overlay Drafting Systems

Chester W. Edwards

McGraw-Hill Book Company
New York   St. Louis   San Francisco   Auckland   Bogotá
Hamburg   Johannesburg   London   Madrid   Mexico City
Montreal   New Delhi   Panama   Paris   São Paulo
Singapore   Sydney   Tokyo   Toronto

*Give credit to architects everywhere who strive
to keep up with villains' murals of ruin by creating
visions of beauty for all of humanity.*

Library of Congress Cataloging in Publication Data

Edwards, Chester W.
  Overlay drafting systems.

  Includes index.
    1. Overlay drafting systems.   2. Structural drawing.
  3. Architectural drawing.   I. Title.
  T352.E37   1984   604.2'4   84-4348
  ISBN 0-07-019047-X

1234567890 KGB/KGB 89875654

ISBN 0-07-019047-X

*The editors of this book were Joan Zseleczky and
Galen H. Fleck; the designer was Naomi Auerbach; and
the production supervisor was Thomas G. Kowalczyk. It
was set in Aster by BPE Graphics.*

Printed and bound by Kingsport Press

Contents

Preface

A story that came out of the Truman-Dewey presidential campaign applies to this book. At one whistlestop, Dewey, who was a famous orator and lawyer, made an impressive speech. It was full of long words and paragraphs. When he had finished, one listener turned to another and said, "Great speech! He sure knows how to talk."

"Yeah, he's terrific," the other replied. "I really like to hear him speak." And after a long pause he added wistfully, "I kinda wish I knew what he was talking about!"

Maybe Dewey lost the election because of a language gap.

A language gap is perhaps the biggest barrier to greater acceptance of overlay drafting. The aim of this book is to bridge that gap, to make plain the meaning of words and terms that are too easily taken for granted by the experts. Most architects, for example, have had their first exposure to overlay drafting from reprographic salespersons. One of those people was to remark, in apparent frustration, that it would be easy to sell overlay if he could only get to the comptroller of the architectural firm.

The language gap extends even beyond that. In a recent publication of a major company the overlay technique was promoted with this statement: "Team drafting—makes it possible to have three or more drafters working on the same project at the same time." That, of course, is hardly a strong selling point to architects who have been using large staffs on projects without the use of systems drafting, overlay technique, or computer-aided design.

"Speaking the language" has different meanings to those promoting pin graphics as a production aid. Some stress time and cost savings; others emphasize technical aspects or the value of color printing. The intent of this book is to point out the importance of the overlay technique as an essential tool for better management, a tool with exceptional potential. The primary target is management, not the drafting force; the effort is to create greater interest in advancing management proficiency. After all, if management cannot be influenced to be reflective and to improve the way things are done, it is unlikely that the overlay technique will have any meaning no matter how valuable some others have found it to be.

A very serious, basic knowledge gap is a genuine concern to managers who are tempted to look into the concept. Here are some examples:

▪ *Who gets helped and who gets the worst of it?* The overlay technique definitely makes the manager's job tougher while making drafting easier.

▪ *The language.* Reproduction people tend toward such lingo as, "We put out great intermediate transparency sepia Mylar overlay reproducibles." Impressive, indeed, but who knows what it means? Someone has to simplify terms. The best way is to stick to elementary process and material terms such as use of "diazo" rather than "sepia transparency."

▪ *The practical.* Centralize reproduction services. An in-house installation is *the* way to go, with commercial services for backup, volume printing, and precise photography. The office with a first-rate reproduction setup has the edge on productivity gains. Start with at least a whiteprinter. Far better is to have both a whiteprinter and a flatbed vacuum frame. These two units, expertly put to use, are the firm basis for *productivity* and *cost savings*.

▪ *What's unusual?* A drafting room in which the overlay technique and a vacuum frame are used will have a great many brown-line tracings floating around. These will be diazo reproductions on polyester film, usually the product of a scissors drafting assembly on a clear acetate or polyester film sheet.

▪ *The diazo drawback.* At present diazo products have short archival life. They age quickly, and they must be copied by more permanent methods which include CAD, large-size copiers and photography, including microfilm. Incidentally, most architects prefer brown-line diazo prints to black-line ones.

▪ *Why is overlay important?* Production is a function of proficiency. The overlay technique is the basis for high-level proficiency, and it is also immediately related to use of the computer in the preparation of construction documents.

▪ *Who gets the architect started?* Be realistic. The learning initiative rests solely with the architect. Reproduction people know equipment, material, methods, and to some extent the overlay technique. But nobody knows drawing production as well as the architect knows it.

▪ *Involve the engineers and consultants.* How? Perhaps by directing them to use the overlay system and, since that is bound to save them money, cut their fees. That might work, but consider another approach. The architect who is knowledgeable about advanced production methods can advise engineers and consultants on organization, planning, scheduling, and sheet planning. That comes first. A good way to go about it is to have lectures for house staff and selected members of the engineers' and consultants' staffs. Lead the engineers into the team.

■ *Precision photography.*   Probably precision photography is underrated and underused by architects because they are unaware of its versatility. This is one area in which most reprographic firms—perhaps the entire industry—fall short of capitalizing on the architect's needs. The process camera-projector units described in Chapter 6 offer broad-value cost-saving shortcuts by enlargement, reduction, restoration, small-negative refinement, and filing. They also will meet the eventual needs of computer output.

Entering into the overlay system can be an enjoyable learning experience that opens the way to a prosperous future.

Chester W. Edwards

Illustrations

CHAPTER ONE

Introduction

The architects who were trying to improve the quality of graphics must have been encouraged to learn about an innovation by which color assumes new importance in architectural practice. Color typically denotes artistic expression, but in its new role it has a unique practical value: it makes possible the "publishing" of construction documents in color. Many architects now have color capability and are producing construction documents of superb quality. And although there are prestige advantages to multicolored drawings, the constructor who is fortunate enough to use such documents must find joy and great relief in being free of the long-enduring, aggravating blueprint.

Colored construction drawings are a long-needed advance, but color is a by-product and not a production development by itself. Color printing has been around for a long time in graphic arts and map making. The architectural development stems from the graphic arts industry, and for architects it is a form of mechanization that leads the way to modern production technology.

Drafting Room Mechanization Mechanization in the drafting room? How can that be; how can anything basic to the factory be fitting to an art? But mechanization of sorts it is, and it has a number of names: overlay system, pin graphics, pin registration, photodrafting, overlay register system, team drafting, multi-image registration. The mechanization aspect centers around the special use of certain items of reproduction equipment and a long, narrow strip of metal called a registration bar or pin bar. The registration, or pin, bar is the unifying element of what has developed as a sophisticated science for the drafting room: the overlay system.

Of course, an expert on modern industrial technology and assembly-line robots might be excused for pointing to that simple strip of metal with a number of round pins fixed to its surface, and asking, "What? You call *that* mechanization?"

Mechanization? Certainly—and badly needed in the design profession for years. It may be difficult to relate to the concept of industrial mechanization, and it may be difficult to identify with elements that, instead of being housed in one facility, are scattered from drafting board to reproduction plant. But no matter the impressions or the doubts, the system does work. Architects are profiting from overlay use, and, in fact, so are those who mastered overlay and then invested in computer installations.

The term "mechanization" may appear too harsh to associate with an artistic profession, but it serves to emphasize a point: "Architects take notice. There *is* a better way." That better way is pin graphics, the modern basis for drafting production. It introduces new terms to be learned: base sheet, overlay, composite, punches, pin bars, polyester film, diazo, vacuum frames.

The *base sheet,* sometimes referred to as the *base,* is in its final form an incomplete drawing. In contrast, a floor plan normally contains a considerable number of dimensions, notes, references, space titles and numbers, and schedules. But such data are kept off the base sheet. Instead, they are placed on one or a series of overlay sheets. Then base sheet and overlays come together in the composite, which is issued as a complete drawing for construction. The process is illustrated by Figures 1-1 to 1-5.

Preparation of the base sheet is restricted to just plan layouts to facilitate drafting progress, produce construction data faster, and minimize gaps in production sequence, that is, to get quicker induction of engineering into project development. The effect is impressive not only on progress but also on quality, since the architect now has more control over the selection and placement of all data during composition of the floor plan base sheet.

After the base sheet has reached a significant point of development, drafting starts on the necessary *overlays.* The overlays contain all the supplemental data necessary to make a final sheet or sheets suitable for use by construction forces. The architectural data on the overlay directly relates to that on the base sheet.

An overlay is always prepared in registration with the base sheet it will complement. *Pin registration* is the standard way to register one sheet to another. It is also used during production of the final version of a construction drawing, the *composite.* Through pin registration, the base sheet and all the overlays relate one to another in the composite, the final print.

The base sheet serves another invaluable purpose: It gives the architect an opportunity to visualize the influence of management, to grasp the significance of the interrelations, of management and drawing production. The architect who is intently working a sheet—absorbed with the demanding task of placing, line by line, words and symbols on a drawing—is hardly going to be concerned with the management factor. That will remain almost a mystery, and little attention will be paid to it.

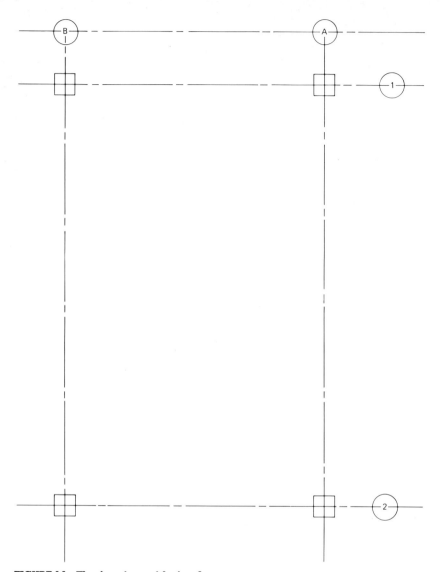

FIGURE 1-1 The framing grid, step 1.

1. The framing grid can be produced by drawing in ink on film, by scribing, by computer plotter, or by a commercial printer.

2. A grid can also be developed further as a structural framing plan.

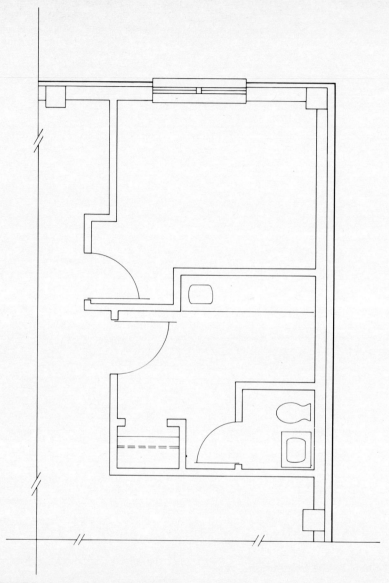

FIGURE 1-2 The base sheet, step 2.

1. The plan, drawn as a base sheet, is restricted to the primary data that guides construction work.

2. A plan in this mode is easier for clients to understand and is easier to change.

3. The base sheet serves as a background layout for engineering design. Engineers do not have to draw plans; they draw only design systems.

4. The technique is the basis for time and cost savings. Consultants have less waiting time before starting, and they spend less time on repetitive drafting. All time and cost savings are money saved *up front*.

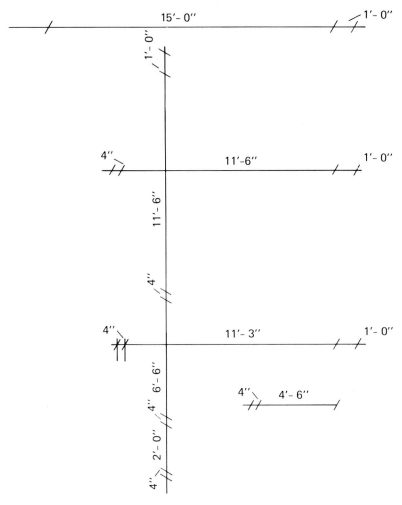

FIGURE 1-3 The dimension overlay, step 3.

1. An overlay is a key simplification device, one of the few available to the design professional.

2. An overlay is defined as containing data relevant to change. For example, dimensions are all that will be shown on a dimension overlay; and when changes in dimension are required, they can be made without altering or disturbing other types of data that do not need to be changed.

3. Each saving in time, no matter how minor, contributes to a project's financial success.

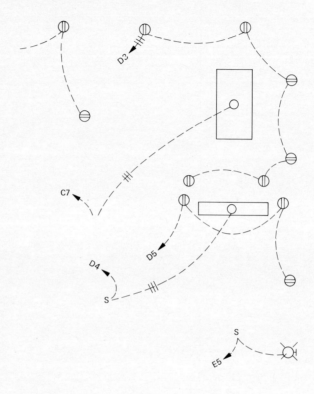

FIGURE 1-4 An engineering overlay, step 4.

1. After the architect proves out the floor plan base sheet, copies of it are made for use as background by the engineers.

2. Only the architect makes changes to plans and is responsible for plan quality. Engineers make no changes in plan; they make only changes in design.

3. The overlay is an engineering system. If it is made available to contractors, it makes pricing of the work easier and also makes systems easier to understand and follow.

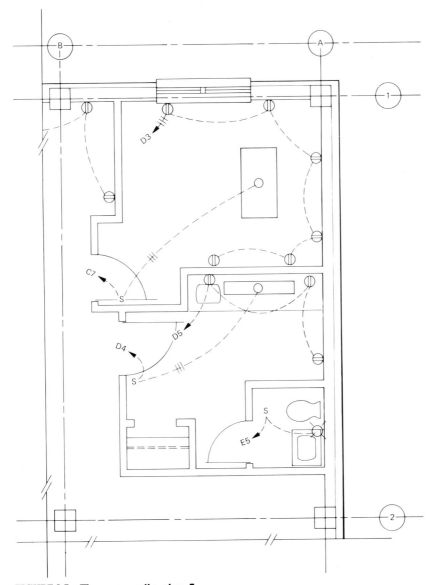

FIGURE 1-5 The composite, step 5.

1. By pin-registering the framing grid, floor plan, and electrical drawing overlay, the composite is produced. It is a complete electrical plan ready for use in construction.

2. This example was produced on a flatbed vacuum frame by the diazo process. A total of three sheets were exposed at the same time in a pin-registered mode.

3. During the reproduction process, the architect also has the option of screening one particular sheet, often the floor plan base sheet. However, when four or more sheets are printed together on a registration bar, the sheet farthest from the emulsion surface will have a screened appearance.

The overlay technique, on the other hand, requires that close attention be given to the demands of management if the results are to be successful. A drawing for construction is not prepared in the same manner as a presentation drawing, which is created almost entirely from instinct and intuition. A construction drawing is prepared within the framework of logic for pricing purposes, for guiding the layout of work, or for guiding the efforts of field forces. Efficient preparation and orderly logical execution are essential. The overlay system offers the architect those opportunities. To most architects, however, management seems like a function that belongs only in the front office. "There's no place for it in the drafting room, no way that a drawing can be produced on an architectural assembly line."

Multicolored drawings for construction, produced through the pin graphics technique, attract attention and identify the progressive professional. But color, the window dressing of design output, is not the main reason for using better ways to produce drawings. Profit is the primary reason, although many architects will say that the improvement in drawing quality is a better one. Actually, the two are not separable; improvement and profit go together. So why are more architects not converting drafting rooms to the overlay system before they get into computer use?

Resistance to New Ways It is natural to be pessimistic and suspicious about revolutionary innovations, and it is easy to visualize the worst—high costs, extraordinary complexity, internal resistance, even disaster. Those are real concerns that cannot easily be dispelled. Yet the architect who is in the business of solving problems, for which a certain degree of professional skill is essential, should have enough confidence to put them in the background. Then it should be possible to get a clearer view of the potential of a technique that finally brings technological advances to the drafting room.

The welfare of the enterprise is the primary concern. Seeking better ways to do things has a direct relation with the outcome of efforts to achieve a stable, secure future. Whenever the architect lacks appreciation of the simple, elementary need for constant appraisal of productivity, with its obvious influence on profitability, there may be a corresponding lack of appreciation of modern management's influence on production whether by the traditional methods or by the modern overlay method.

It is wrong to presume that the art of architecture must rule the entire production process from design concept to bidding. From a practical stand-point, the art of architecture really ends when the client buys the design. The stage is then set to gear up the project and draw on the production resources of people, equipment, and material. Distinct emphasis is on two essentials, production and management—up-to-date production technology under the administration of expert management. Or so everyone likes to think!

The Value of Expert Management The phrase "expert management" no doubt means different things to different people, particularly when the role of management is weighed against the art of architecture in practice. Preoccupation with design tends to conceal the substance of management, which scholars accept as being both an art and a science. That makes it a proper, useful complement to the ambitious but practical goals of the art of architecture. Figure 1–6 illustrates the predominance of management in all practice activities even though design is usually viewed as primarily an intuitive problem-solving process.

If the appeal of management is lost on designers, it should not be. Mastering the art of management, in particular the skills essential to production is actually less demanding than the effort expended on a design charrette. Just as with the overlay system, there are few obstacles to overcome; there are no patents, no copyrights, and no franchise fees to contend with. On the contrary, there is nothing but encouragement to be met with; for all the important management principles have already been defined by scholars and proved beyond doubt in practice. There is little reason for any architect to reject another art and science with all its potential.

The background of modern management is relevant not only to industry but also to the design profession. The modern industrial era, which began in about 1890, was marked by the changeover from handcrafted manufacture to factory mass production. Right at the beginning, the revolution was in trouble. Managers found they were unprepared for the increasingly complex problems of growth, change, technology, production, and people. Among the executives

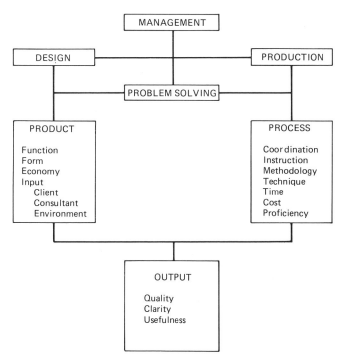

FIGURE 1-6 Architectural practice.

of the time were those who recognized the need for specialized training and knowledge to practice the new profession of management. The result of their perception was the science of management as it is known today: a social science based on a body of principles, a system of practices.

Pioneers of Management Science   The five outstanding pioneers of management were Frederick W. Taylor, Henry L. Gantt, Harrison Emerson, and Frank and Lillian Gilbreth. The latter were the subjects of an inspiring and humorous book written by their children that was later made into the delightful motion picture *Cheaper by the Dozen.* Together these influential leaders presented over ninety principles that are as valid today as they were when first offered. Many apply only to industrial management, but others are entirely applicable to the design profession. They have been ignored too long.

Frederick W. Taylor, who wrote *Principles of Scientific Management* in 1911, initiated basic management philosophy with four principles:

1. Use scientific work methods rather than leave work methods to the judgment of individual workers.

2. Use scientific methods for the selection and training of workers.

3. Cooperation between management and workers is essential for solving problems and for getting work done efficiently.

4. Work should be divided according to ability, education, and experience.

Along with advances in management philosophy came the development of tools of management to make the new science function successfully and efficiently. One of them was invented by H. L. Gantt, a Taylor associate. It was the bar chart production schedule from which evolved today's complex scheduling systems: CPM, PERT, Logical Sequencing.

AIA Awareness of Financial Problems   The art of architecture preceded both mechanized industry and the art of management, but, somewhat unprepared like the industrial age, architecture entered an era in which it was to encounter new and complex problems serious enough to threaten the profitability of a practice. The initial response to this threat was not by individuals, but by the American Institute of Architects. In 1968 a series of studies produced advisory reports such as "Emerging Trends in Architectural Programming," "The Economics of Architectural Practice," and "Profit Planning in Architectural Practice." The following are some of the important points worth emphasizing here:

1. One of twelve firms and one of four projects lost money.

2. Architects get little formal training in business administration, make little effort to acquire the training, and generally do not recognize the benefits to be gained from good business practices.

3. Architects are not nearly as effective in administration as they are in design, and they are not responding as efficiently as might be desired to the challenges of administration problems.

Primarily, the AIA reports emphasized the need for improved administration in practice, and that need has not changed. But lacking in all the reports was any comprehensive interpretation of the essentials that early pioneers insisted were badly needed by managers, whether industrial or architectural.

Basic theory has guided managers through the years, but right from the very beginning there apparently was one principle that very few managers could understand and put into practice. That most crucial principle was Taylor's *cooperation.* For many years the subject of cooperation received little attention, and few attempts were made to create some appreciation for the principle until 1960. Then interest in cooperation was revived by scholar Douglas McGregor with his book *The Human Side of Enterprise,* published by McGraw-Hill.

Principle of Cooperation McGregor's work produced some controversy, but it drew attention to the significant potential cooperation would have in all future management thinking. McGregor accused contemporary management of not fully realizing the potential of people and of improper assumptions about human nature. He illustrated the latter with his famous Theory X and Theory Y. He presented values about people which were somewhat widely held but had never been deeply examined or clearly stated before. Theory X, for example, detailed management's long-held ideas about people that McGregor insisted were in error. Theory Y examined the attitudes that management should have if it wanted to get employee cooperation. People, he said, make commitments to achieve an organization's goals not because they are directed to do so, but for reasons of individual pride, personal satisfaction, recognition, and perhaps just the fun of it.

No matter how persuasive it may be, a theory has to have convincing proof, and that has been appearing. Already three books strongly support McGregor. Robert Townsend, as president of Avis, may have been one of the first to apply McGregor's views to the management of a major business. In his book *Up the Organization* (Knopf, 1970) Townsend writes, "If I had anything to do with [Avis' success], I ascribe it all to my application of [McGregor's] Theory Y!"

McGregor promoted the theme of cooperation by presenting a scholar's views about human nature to management. On the other hand, William W. Caudill of Caudill Rowlett Scott, a prominent architect and pioneer in advanced practice technique, explained the way management, by placing complete confidence in people, used the team concept to achieve cooperation and commitment. His book *Architecture by Team* (Van Nostrand Reinhold, 1971) is more than a new version of practice; it is another important statement of management principles. For architectural purposes it is as profound as McGregor's work. It gives answers to basic questions that perplex students as much as experienced architects. Just how do you manage a project? How do you manage a practice? The answers have been needed for a long time.

Human resources—the foundation for productivity—are apparently understood by Japanese managers, whose appreciation of the "human side of enterprise" is receiving so much notice from American businessmen and writers. One of them, William Ouchi, probed the Japanese style of management in depth. As he wrote in *Theory Z* (Addison-Wesley, 1981), he interpreted the Japanese management philosophy as built around these fundamentals:

Productivity Worked out through coordination of individual efforts to achieve the long-range view.

Trust Employee sacrifices will be rewarded.

Subtlety Managers learn weaknesses, pinpoint personalities, and find who works well with whom to put together an effective team.

Although architects may take good care of their clients' interests, their own best interests deserve the same close attention and care of planning if they are to meet the challenge of assignments that grow in complexity and size. The formula for success is not clearly definable, but the following elements can be detected in the practice of leading firms:

1. Business development
2. Profit planning
3. Personnel growth
4. Management training
5. Management tools
6. Production tools, such as the overlay system

Just as industry has its pioneers, so the design profession has its leaders in practice innovation and technology. What is so heartening is the wealth of generous attitudes and the encouraging of others to catch up and contribute to progress. Some of the leaders who deserve a great deal of credit are Ned Abrams, Phil Bennett, William W. Caudill, Gary Gerlach, Donald Jarvis, Jerry Quebe, Fred A. Stitt, and Herbert C. Wheeler, Jr.

CHAPTER TWO

The Overlay System

Choices open to the production-minded architect get better all the time. To the traditional method of hand drafting two other basic production methods have been added. They are computer-aided design (CAD) and the overlay-register technique often called pin graphics. From a practical standpoint, all three are directly related. Conventional hand drafting will be around for a long time, and it is essential for the overlay system. Also, experience is demonstrating that the combination of the overlay system, hand drafting, and CAD can provide a highly effective production system.

Origin of the Technique The origin of the overlay-register technique is somewhat hazy. Legend has it that, shortly after World War II, the U.S. Army Corps of Engineers experimented with a scribe coat technique that involved applying a thin even coat of tar by hand to a sheet of glass. After the tar dried, lines were inscribed through it with a sharp knife.

The next step was the radical departure of registering different drawings or sheets, a basic technique still in use today. The modern version is covered in a Corps of Engineers publication issued in 1961: Technical Manual TB353, "The Overlay-Composite Method of Master Plan Preparation." This manual appears to be the first publication on the overlay technique; it has detailed descriptions of fundamentals, materials, registration, and procedures. Except for registration methods, most of it remains valid today.

Negative Engraving Another manual, Technical Bulletin TB353-1, "Preparation of Master Plans by Negative Engraving and Type Overlay Techniques," is best suited to cartography, but architects and engineers may have occasional use for the concept. Negative engraving is performed on a sheet of scribe-coated material. The actinically opaque coating, or emulsion, is factory-applied to a sheet of suitable material such as stable-base polyester film. It is thin and easily cut or scribed with a sharp needle or cutting tool. Scribing or cutting a line merely removes the coating without damaging the clear base film material. The result of scribing, the negative engraving, is similar to a photographic negative which produces sharp lines and images. According to Manual TB353-1,

> It is generally conceded to produce quality superior to the best ink drafted positive (tracing). The base material is transparent, and the actinically opaque emulsion on the scribe coat is removed during the scribing procedures so that during the photographic processes, light passing through the scribed line will pass through with absolute equal intensity to produce lines of consistent intensity. Conversely, the variations in density of an ink drafted line are obvious when magnified. Variation that is caused by lack of absolute opacity of ink, variations in drafting material and drafting, technique and ability.

Interestingly, TB353-1 points out,

> A scriber with just two months of training is capable of producing work superior in quality to that of a draftsman using ink who has two years of training. Also, normally, scribing is 20 to 30 percent faster than ink drafting since there are no instruments to be filled with ink and none to be cleaned.

The production techniques of the scribe coat process are;

1. By photographic or diazo processes, scribing an image such as an aerial photo recorded on a scribe coat to which has been added a light-sensitive emulsion. After development of this sensitized coating the scriber engraves the necessary lines and images such as buildings, railroads, and water.

2. By tracing, using a light table and transparent copy material for copying by scribing.

3. By scribing lines previously drawn by hand, pencil, or ink on the surface of the scribe coat material.

Another comment about scribing appeared in the November 1975 issue of *Engineering Graphics:*

> One of the most successful drafting developments to come along in recent years is scribe coat film. Incised lines of the scribe coat do not vary in width, cannot be smudged and are generally much more accurate than their inked counterparts. Further, extremely sharp prints can be produced directly from scribe coat origi-nals. Some users report time savings of almost one third on very close tolerance drawings over other methods.... There is a prevailing trend toward scribing.

Negative engraving, although capable of producing work of superior quality, can be an extremely complex production system. The necessary know-how and proficiency do require a special investment. Since TB353-1 was issued, the great potential of the overlay technique has been realized in such fields as building design, ship design, printed-circuit-board layout, and product manufacture. For architects, one of the most sophisticated versions of the overlay technique, with emphasis on organization and project planning, appeared in the February 1975 issue of the *Journal of the American Institute of Architects* in an article by Jerry Quebe, AIA Principal of Hansen, Lind, Meyers, Architects.

Development Centered on New Materials   The overlay system came about as a two-part development. The original idea of registration for development of construction drawings had one weakness at the beginning. Early experimenters had only glass and paper to work with, and neither was an ideal match with the registration requirements for precise accuracy. Glass was just too impractical; and paper has extremely poor dimensional stability, which makes composite registration unreliable as well as inaccurate. Thus, enthusiasm for the new idea was dampened.

In 1951, interest in the overlay system began to revive when the Du Pont Company introduced a new flexible plastic sheet material that was perfectly compatible with the technique. The new material, a polyester-base film manufactured in large roll and sheet sizes, was well suited to both drafting and reproduction purposes. It could be produced with a matte surface that would take pencil and ink and also with photographic emulsions for the reproduction industry. The prospects for change looked brighter.

Why use the overlay system, is it for every office? To find an answer, put aside thoughts of architecture for the moment and consider the three P's of practice: *positive, productivity,* and *profit.*

Positive   Attitude means everything in the application of any new development. A negative, show-me attitude gets the prospective user nowhere. It is unnecessary to prove the system; that's being done. The proper attitude to take is, "We want to keep up to date, how can we put the system into use for our firm?"

Productivity   Probably the most serious disadvantage of the traditional hand-drafting method is that attempts at simplification and standardization are resisted. Traditionally, every drafter feels free to develop individualistic, special ways of doing things. They may be skilled, efficient ways or crude, primitive, costly ways; everything depends on the individual's ability. Many architects, of course, are fully capable of effective production and can make a profit on every job, but their ways may not work for others.

Profit   A well-proven principle of management is that a team is more effective than any group of unorganized individuals. The team is the key to productivity; the system is the invaluable tool that facilitates management success. A team does not function effectively if each member uses a different production method. The team concept has in its favor a firmer control of efforts, principally the individualistic efforts of team members, without curbing creativity and originality. It is not always a simple matter to visualize consequences of good management (and money in the bank), and of incidental management that may endanger profitability, as illustrated in Figure 2-1.

Involvement with Overlays Is the overlay system for every office? The answer is yes for every office involved with the production of drawings for construction. The small-office architect may wonder at that, but the advice is still the same. Get involved; become proficient; and be better prepared to face the challenges of the future. The overlay system changes the production of drawings from a demanding task to a more interesting and creative one.

How to produce graphic documentation in the best possible form to suit the purposes of the builder (not the drafter, as so many seem to think) and place proper emphasis on the design effort is a troublesome problem to those responsible for design and drafting production. The overlay system is, of course, directed at drafting production. But it offers productive support for the design element while recognizing that drawing production is both a business matter and a professional and technical one.

The overlay system has two distinct elements. Production within the drafting room, and production processes within the reproduction plant. For that reason it is essential that the design professional become knowledgeable about the advances being made in reproduction services that can benefit the design professional, the drafter, the builder, and the project owner.

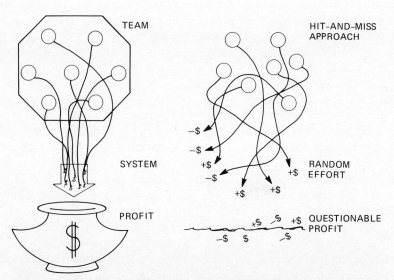

FIGURE 2-1 Drafting room concepts. When the team is organized and the job is planned, scheduled, and coordinated, the result is profit. When a hit-and-miss approach is used, the effort is random, funds are dissipated, and profit is questionable.

CHAPTER THREE

Analysis of the System

For those architects with pin bars "hanging in closets," the overlay system must have been a failure, its potential never appreciated, its benefits never realized.

Why should the system fail a user?

There are disadvantages to the system, although they are heavily outweighed by the advantages. Perhaps the user for whom the system failed never realized that it needs special understanding before its introduction to the drafting room. The following may appear to be serious obstacles to success of the overlay system, but regular system users have had little trouble accommodating to them. Perhaps they took the time to analyze each and every problem to judge its impact on productivity.

SYSTEM DISADVANTAGES

Costs of Training   Every business experiences a need for training personnel. Some firms get by without ever budgeting the needed expense and then wonder why they cannot keep up with others. For example, a certain amount of expense is involved in teaching a new person, usually a recent graduate, how to master complex wall section details. The cost of teaching someone the overlay technique is probably a lot less and is probably a more worthwhile investment. The other part of this problem, of course, is who is going to do the teaching? The answers include having a member of the firm attend seminars and calling in a consultant such as another architect or a qualified reproduction specialist.

Fragmentation of a Project The basis for the fragmentation problem is likely to be complainers or lack of advance planning that results in confused people, duplication of effort, and staff downtime when people run out of work. Here is where Taylor's principle of cooperation applies. A briefing of all staff members should emphasize the newness of the idea and the opportunity to learn, advance, and profit. Someone must take the lead in putting the system into effect and be able to delegate responsibility to achieve greatest possible participation.

Complexity of the System The unique thing about the overlay system is its ability to be as simple or complex as the architect wants it to be. A composite, the complete drawing for construction, might be nothing more than an architectural floor plan as the base sheet and a lighting plan as the overlay. Together they form the electrical engineer's lighting plan. On the other hand, a complex product would be a floor plan base sheet plus an overlay for a ceiling grid, another for room names, another for a lighting plan, and another for emergency lighting. The key is to make the system work by keeping everything as simple as possible to begin with; it appears complex when it is not thoroughly understood. First concentrate on the fundamentals, including the equipment and the materials involved with the system. Keep in mind most of the overlay technique involves floor plan layouts; that alone should reduce the fear of complexities.

First-Time Mistakes Thorough briefing and planning are essential for keeping first-time mistakes to a minimum. Examples of such mistakes are using a 3-mil instead of a 4-mil sheet, starting a drawing on a sheet that has not been punched, drawing on the back side of a sheet, and trying to use paper tracings or paper prints in the production process.

Coordination of Sheet Data The problem of coordinating sheet data involves the drawing number, key plan, north arrows, room names and numbers, dimensions, and notes. Sheet model layouts help reduce coordination problems.

Extra Planning Effort Is extra planning really a problem? The important consideration is that the overlay system does require planning the project carefully. But if extra planning effort is made an issue, then the question is whether any planning is ever done. In fact, planning a project for traditional production methods centered around hand drafting has been a typical office weakness.

More Sheets to Handle and Store The thing to remember about handling and storing sheets is that the additional sheets are in some ways special assets. They may take a little more time and effort to handle, store, and file, but their special potential for fast-track projects, brochures, as-built drawings, and shop drawings should make all that worthwhile.

High Reproduction Costs Although costs can get out of hand, the architect not only has some means of control but should relate reproduction expenses to the savings achieved through use of the system. System operating costs include the following, and the architect must take a close look at each item to see how it can be controlled.

- Stable base sheets for in-house drafting purposes and for consultants
- Punching of sheets
- Reproduced base sheets for consultant use; usually throwaways
- Method of reproduction for base sheets and for composites: flat-bed printer or camera-projector (the most expensive way)
- Check printing for client and consultant
- Pin bars for in-house and consultant use

EFFECT ON PRODUCTIVITY

The overlay system is sound in principle and well proven in practice. Some may question the wisdom of separating information on different sheets, and sometimes the cost of preparing a drawing in the conventional way will be less than that of doing it by the overlay method. Total production efficiency, however, is the main objective of the overlay system. It is a function of the critical factors in productivity: initial drafting effort, erasing mistakes, redrawing changed work, repetitive drawing, and coordination between in-house staff and consultants.

With the overlay system the architect can tackle unusual and difficult production problems and achieve solutions not possible in any other way, except perhaps via the computer. The system does require a strictly disciplined effort lest traditional habits make it a casualty of carelessness. Attempts to stray from fundamentals should be anticipated from the start and kept under control. Education and training of staff on every aspect of the system is elementary and is vital to successful use and enjoyment of benefits.

Growth When considering the benefits to be gained from something new, the growth factor cannot be overlooked. Is the system susceptible to future improvement or will it go out of date? There is little chance the traditional hand production method can be improved from its present state; and there is less chance it can survive the competition of the overlay technique, let alone that of the combination of overlay technique and CAD, the new pin graphics.

An architect may feel comfortable with traditional production methods if the office staff consists of people who have been working well together over a period of time. Such a team of sorts, not identified as such, can have a high level of expertness for certain types of projects. One member may be expert at plans; another may put out beautiful elevations; another may whip out construction details. But if no preparation is made for change, the unexpected happens. A complex job is taken on; consultants are called in; someone quits;

someone goes on vacation; a new, inexperienced person comes aboard; and things are no longer the same and production suddenly declines. Add to this the fact that other members of the project—site, structural, mechanical, and electrical engineers—may all be employing different production methods and reducing the effectiveness of the production effort. Acceptance of the overlay system begins with a clear understanding of what can be gained from it.

SYSTEM ADVANTAGES

Control of Plan Quality   Use of the overlay system ensures that plans that are the basis for ceiling layouts, interior planning, and engineering layouts will be identical in appearance, accuracy, and quality. The reason is that only the architect draws plans and only the architect makes plan changes. That should be made clear to project engineers who use floor plans for reference purposes. They will do their work only on overlays, and they do not make changes in floor plan base sheets. All of their productive output applies to their particular elements of work: design of systems.

Improved Drawing Quality   Some drawings, such as floor plans, take a great deal of working over during the development process, and quality often suffers. The data separation technique, by the use of individually prepared base sheets and overlays, spreads the drafting effort over two or more sheets. As a result, there are fewer lines and words to be drawn and written, erased, and redrawn. Working over a sheet is substantially reduced, and quality is assured.

Economics of drawing changes   Precision changing is another advantage of the overlay system. There will seldom be the need, so often found in conventional drafting, to remove some item of information and then redraw it on the sheet in its original state simply because it happened to be adjacent to an item that had to be changed for good reason. The importance of precision changing is underscored by the demands of financial management. Drafting should be a positive action as much as possible; erasing is a negative action. Money is made only on drafting that is accomplished, not on the erasing that takes place. Keep erasing to a minimum and sheets will be worked over less, remain cleaner, and print with better clarity.

Preparation technique   Another aspect of quality is directly related to the principle of data separation. When a drafter prepares a drawing in the conventional way, a floor plan, for example, the plan must be worked to completion no matter how greatly the information to be placed on the drawing has been underestimated. If an error in judgment is serious and erasing and redrawing take place, the result may be a drawing of such poor quality that the field forces for whom it is intended find it difficult to read. Its value as a communication device has been reduced. Quality is no longer assured.

With the overlay technique, quality can be controlled with more precision. Base sheets and overlays can be composited in any manner to meet any standard of quality. If, for example, one base sheet and a number of overlays when combined together in a test printing are judged to produce a drawing of substandard quality or excessive congestion occurs, the components can be separated into different combinations of final drawings of higher caliber. No additional hand production is needed; all is handled by the reproduction services. The composites, the final drawings, are those that best serve the interests of the constructors.

Professional liability concerns The overlay approach to quality control has some professional liability implications. Serious claims against architects and engineers are centered around drawing errors and omissions. The overlay technique provides better ways to combat problems of drawing quality and reduce errors, conflicts, and risks. Here is one example:

A sprinkler system is a project responsibility; accurate layout may be critical to the actual installation. By the conventional drafting method, the system is likely to be drawn on the same sheet as a piping layout. If the drawing has a great amount of detail, some of the sprinkler system detail is in danger of being obscured by other detail when the drawing is printed. By the overlay method, on the other hand, the sprinkler system would be drawn on a separate overlay. To make certain there were no conflicts or any danger to quality, the sprinkler system overlay could be combined with any other overlay and base sheet to obtain a composite drawing. Once again, the technique does not require any additional handwork expense on the part of the architect or engineer.

The decision to individualize an important system is a managerial one influenced by the availability of the overlay system and its unique capability to function as an effective problem-solving tool.

Smoother Project Development Drawings such as floor plans, when drawn as base sheets on prepunched polyester-base drafting film, are limited to illustrating construction layout information. They are:

- Easier to create.
- Clearer to read. Progress review is facilitated, especially when those not experienced in drawing production or construction are involved in the planning process.
- Easier to change and modify.

Precision changing also contributes to efficiency of the team effort. Since changes to drawings, base sheets, and overlays can be made in less time, they can be communicated to other team members more quickly. Once basic layout information is changed, it is not necessary to wait for all supplemental data to be changed. The basic drawing, with its changed data, can be printed and distributed to team members for individual follow-up action. By this production technique, the elapsed project development time is reduced, which in turn helps schedule deadlines to be met. Schedule deadlines mandate getting engineers and consultants involved as soon as possible. That means concentrating initial production efforts on developing the information that engineers need for design and computations and planning information that precedes poché, notes, space names, dimensions, and other architectural data. Start-up data for engineers include exterior walls, interior partitions, columns, floor openings for stairs, elevators, and shafts, slabs that are raised, depressed, or sloped, curbs, pits, and trenches. The architect will need input from the engineers regarding the earliest they can get involved in production and exactly what is needed.

Better Coordination It is usually convenient to establish regular timing points for coordination of architects, engineers, and consultants. But the real truth is that only one person is responsible for coordination, and that is the project manager. Although a certain amount of responsibility can be delegated to subordinate staff members, coordination will be much more successful when the manager constantly monitors the job and progress right from the beginning. Another word for coordination might be "monitoring"; for without constant monitoring of progress and activity, a project can easily slip, almost unnoticed, into trouble.

The best management tool for coordination, through use of the overlay system, is the study of a combination of drawings either by use of a light table, which would require either originals or reproducibles, or composite white-prints. An early coordination effort, for example, would be to guarantee that each engineer has the proper base sheet to start work with. It is not uncommon to have an engineer working on a data sheet that is not the latest issue.

Uniform Drawing Development The overlay system offers an improvement of the drawing process to provide better organization of a project, particularly in regard to putting together certain complex or cluttered sheets. Overlay techniques and methods provide ways to sequence and position information to reinforce the concept of the team. As development planning is implemented, or even as changes are formalized during production, any number of staff personnel can be assigned to a particular drawing to speed up its completion. One person works a layout, another the dimensions, another the space names and numbers. This technique is often referred to by reproduction specialists as having more than one person work on the same drawing.

Better Screening Quality Screening lines or images has certain advantages. It is often useful to tone down the layout of a floor plan, as background data, so that primary layout data will read stronger. Such data might be a lighting plan, ductwork, or piping. Screening is a reproduction technique for reducing line strength by interposing a manufactured product, a fine-screen film, between negative and positive in photographic or diazo contact reproduction. Screens are available in a wide range of fine-lined grids identified by ratings that range from 20 to 70 percent. The figure indicates how much of the line strength remains on the reproduction.

Screening problems As a reproduction procedure, screening can be a source of real trouble when used with traditional drafting methods. One common screening misuse is to furnish engineers with photographic copies of the architectural floor plan. Such sheets are usually wash-off film, and they are intended for direct drafting by the engineers who receive them. The object is to save the engineers the work and expense of drafting a plan by hand.

The technique is useful and cost-saving up to a certain point: that at which it becomes necessary to change the plan. Then drawing quality and efficiency begin to deteriorate. In addition to the architect, each and every consultant must make identical corrections to an individual version of the plan. If the reproducible that is furnished is a reverse-read copy (in which the photographic image is on the back side of the sheet), changing means picking the sheet up off the board, turning it over, and erasing on the back. This correction procedure is slow enough in any case, but the time expense builds up rapidly when wash-off lines are erased. The expense factor worsens drastically if a two-part chemical is required for line removal. Then, after corrections are made, the drawing must be picked up again and turned over, and the changes must be hand-drafted on the front side. This expensive process can become devastating on a project with a large number of architectural and engineering floor plans.

Changing screened lines Another serious problem arises from an attempt to change screened lines. Matching the strength of a screened line by hand drafting is difficult and time-consuming. The problem worsens when changes occur regularly and different people work the drawing. The usual result is that line strength becomes somewhat ridiculous. Screened lines stay screened at a certain strength, and hand repairs of changed lines then print either lighter or darker. Plan quality suffers badly as repairs make the drawing take on a patchy look.

There is another factor involved in image line screening. When full-size drawings are photographically created with image lines screened and a decision is made to print by offset for construction purposes, the drawings are often reduced, usually to half size. When that is done, the screened lines of the original drawing will become extremely light and will often actually vanish from the print. When that happens, of course, it becomes almost impossible to repair any lines.

With the overlay system, screening is principally a function of reproduction; it is fit properly into routine project procedures. It is performed only when needed—occasionally for check printing or for final printing whether by diazo or offset. The screening takes place only at that time; consequently there are none of the problems encountered with screening used during conventional production. Another advantage of screening with the overlay system is the ability to change screen strengths at any time; at worst, there is a minor reproduction expense. If a screened image is considered too light or too dark, it can easily be changed to a more appropriate line strength on another reproduction. Again the only expense is reproduction.

More Useful Status Reporting Scheduling for time and cost control requires that there be some means of establishing job status. Some managers are satisfied with monitoring progress merely to the extent of project phases or groups of drawings. A more precise way is to monitor each and every drawing on the job, and then a way to estimate the status of a drawing must be developed. With the overlay system, the precise monitoring of each base and overlay sheet is encouraged simply by establishing a value for each sheet that makes up a final composited drawing. For example, a floor plan base sheet when completed might have an assumed value of 70 percent, the dimension overlay 20 percent, and notes and space identification 10 percent.

Another method is to break down assembly data more extensively and disregard base and overlay divisions: layout, 60 percent; dimensions, 8 percent; notes, 8 percent; title block data, 2 percent; references, 2 percent; and checking effort, 5 percent. Standard reporting methods are a way to improve management skills while lessening management burdens.

Flexibility Features

Bidding alternates Overlay techniques give management new latitude in preparing drawings of the project features the client wants to be priced separately as alternates. These usually late decisions are certain to increase pressure on schedules and to add production problems. The first major problem is how the architect can piece out the alternates and prepare the drawings without suffering any financial loss; the second is how to create drawings that clearly spell out the scope of the work. With the overlay system, the construction features to be priced separately are drawn on one or more overlays, depending on the number of elements of work involved. All are registered with a primary base sheet, which usually will be a floor plan. The bid alternate drawing or drawings will be a composite of the base sheet and overlays of work to be added, changed, or deleted.

Phased construction In fast-track construction management projects, primary use for the overlay system will be similar to that of the bidding alternate issue of drawings. "Fast track" usually means releasing certain drawings earlier than others to get materials on order and construction underway before production of the entire set of construction documents has been completed. By using base sheets and overlays, it is possible to package project data to better fit the scheduling and grouping of separate package contracts.

Better Production Efficiency A worthwhile system improves on old ways of doing things and offers substantial cost benefits as well. Value analysis of drafting systems is difficult to accomplish because there is no simple, easy basis for comparison. Cost saving claims are quite general; one claim may be a saving of anywhere from 30 to 65 percent when repetitive drafting is involved. Another claim is that consultants and engineers may draw about 35 to 40 percent less. On the other hand are those system users who look not at savings, but at opportunities to make better use of design effort or services for clients.

One approach to evaluation of production methods is to compare the costs of producing a drawing by using square foot cost factors. This method is usually an in-house comparison of previous projects for the purpose of setting standards for types of job, not for comparing different systems. The overlay drafting system on the other hand, provides a way to compare the productivity of conventional ways with that of the overlay system. As that way is described here, it relates primarily to the development of floor plans, a project's most fundamental element.

The floor plan is vulnerable to such various adverse factors as time pressures, distractions, interruptions, errors, weaknesses in communication, and inadequate management. Such factors can build up during the development process to such an extent that reworking the plan actually amounts to recreating the drawing more than once by the time it is ready for final printing.

Evaluation methods If the term "plan activity" is applied to the redrawing process, hypothetical evaluation factors can be determined. Table 3-1 illustrates the following explanation of an evaluation example: A plan that is drawn only once during the entire development of a project may be assigned a plan activity factor of 1.0. The factor indicates the production effort needed to get the drawing complete without any change during the production process. A factor of more than 1.0, such as 1.5, would indicate a drawing that incurred minor but significant changes during production, and a drawing with many changes might be rated as much as 2.0.

Although the purpose of a rating system is to find the cost-benefit factor, the subject of who will actually pay for changes has to be given some thought.

For the model shown in Table 3-1 two assumptions concerning conventional drafting practices must be made:

1. The architect and all engineers and consultants will draw complete floor plans.

2. The architect and all engineers and consultants will hand-draft all changes to the floor plans.

In actual practice, however, many firms now use some effective shortcuts such as furnishing photocopies of floor plans to engineers and consultants for hand drafting of special designs and systems. In traditional production methods the architect has the responsibility to draw floor plans; the engineers and consultants draw only systems. Moreover, in the absence of an overlay production technique, each and every member of the team is committed to making changes on the floor plan copy each is using. This factor has the most critical influence on productivity, and the following comparison shows how much that can mean to drafting efficiency.

Plan activity factor assumed, 2.0
Design elements, assumed to be nine per floor:

Floor plan	1
Interior planning	1
Ceiling plan	1
Piping layouts	2
Ductwork	1
Electrical work	2
Communication	1
Total	9

TABLE 3-1 Production Efficiency Comparison
□ Hand-drafted plan; ⌐ ¬ reference copy of plan

Plan	Number of Plans		
	Overlay Method	Conventional Method	
Architectural			
Floor plan	[1] 1	1	[1]
Reflected ceiling plan	[2] 0	1	[2]
Interior planning	[3] 0	1	3
Total plan requirements	1	3	
Plan activity factor, assumed	×2	×2	
Total plan requirements	2	6	
Production efficiency ratio	$\dfrac{2}{6}$		
Engineering			
Plumbing	[4] 0	1	[4]
Sprinkler	[5] 0	1	[5]
Ductwork—supply return	[6] 0	1	[6]
Lighting	[7] 0	1	[7]
Power	[8] 0	1	[8]
Communications	[9] 0	1	[9]
Total plan requirements	0	6	
Plan activity factor, assumed	×2	×2	
Total plan requirements	0	12	
Production efficiency ratio	$\dfrac{0}{12}$		
Totals			
Total plan requirements per floor	1	9	
Times plan activity factor, assumed	×2	×2	
Total plan activities per floor	2	18	
Production efficiency ratio	$\dfrac{2}{18}$		

Other factors involved in the cost-benefit picture are the total number of floors in the project and hourly wages.

WHO BENEFITS?

The overlay system protects the architect's profit factor, although on the surface it would appear that engineers and consultants benefit more than the architect does. The architect's benefits gained from use of the system are not so visible. They accumulate all the way through a project, and most of them have an indirect, positive influence on profit. Extraordinary versatility is probably the most obvious advantage. For example, a single floor plan base sheet has the potential for serving successively as a background for engineering layouts, as an overhead transparency for conferences, in a promotion brochure, for a building renovation, for bid takeoff, for a shop drawing, for as-builts, for a client's plan changes after construction is complete, for changing dimensions to metric, and for changing to a different language—all from one base sheet! The enterprising architect ought to be able to promote such advantages to his own advantage.

The Architect-Publisher But all these advantages come down to just one final, logical argument. The system makes it possible for the graphics art professional to be a publisher—in color. But hasn't the architect always been in the publishing business? Use of the overlay-register technique finally brings the architect in line with the experts of the graphics art industries, who could not stay in business if they put out their polished publications by using archaic production methods like those to which architects have stubbornly clung for so many years.

CHAPTER FOUR

Production Efficiency

The fundamental need of drafting departments for high-level efficiency has been generally accepted, but attempts to revitalize productivity have, until recently, been limited to minor changes in well-known shortcuts. One such technique, scissors drafting, has been in use since before 1918. Such techniques have proven value, but the inability to extend improvement works against the wisdom of putting too much emphasis on the importance of a shortcut as a foundation for productivity.

The overlay system, in contrast, has a subtle relationship with art, requires know-how to produce results, has strength of a creative pursuit, places unqualified reliance on management (another art), and requires considerable understanding of the underlying science that makes it possible. Knowledge of important materials, equipment, and methods employed in allied professions permitted pioneering executives to reevaluate traditional ways of producing drawings for construction and manufacture, which led to the inevitable breakthrough to the better way.

Theory: A Practical Approach That long-delayed evolution of progress graduated into a drafting room science centered on theory and technology and aimed toward the ultimate in drafting room production. Without the benefit of some theory, drawing production, from the manager's standpoint, would be little more than rule-of-thumb practice with improvisations that are often only reflex actions for problem solving. Theory is examined here, but emphasis is again on management ability; for although theory may stimulate managerial thinking, managers rely primarily on knowledge and experience with productive tools to expand proficiency.

Theory is rational explanation of such functions of management as recognizing drawing development as an exercise in logistics. That is, the number of items of information to be placed on any drawing multiplied by the number of sources of information represents the prime effort required to produce a complete, professional drawing. The efficient working of any drawing is also dictated by the routines of all those involved and by the manner in which data is collected, analyzed, and recorded. Drawing speed and drafting shortcuts are not first essentials of drafting productivity. Knowledge of the product and drafting skill are first requirements. The key, of course, is the well-organized person.

An example Here is an example of the manner in which logistics influences production, although it might be viewed as being more applicable to planning than logistics. A drafter, after finishing work on a project, is assigned to another project. He—it could be she—reports to the project manager, who happens to be hard at work on a board developing one of the project drawings. The new drafter is welcomed and directed to get started on a drawing. Without a thought about additional instruction, the drafter gets a sheet of tracing paper, takes it back to his work station, tapes the sheet down on the board, stamps a standard office title block on it, picks up a scale in one hand and a pencil in the other, a look of eagerness shining on his face, and waits and waits and waits!

Finally, embarrassed over the lack of attention paid to him, the drafter approaches the project manager again and reports that he has a sheet of paper on the board and is ready to go. The architect directs the drafter to start working a floor plan for the Eastern School on Oak Street and gives him a set of preliminary drawings. Taking these back to his board, he begins drawing. After some progress, he returns to consult with the architect and notices that his supervisor is doing his drafting on a preprinted format sheet.

Taken aback, he returns to his board, removes the tracing with a fair amount of work already recorded on it, discards it, gets a new format sheet, and starts all over again. Later, after working the second sheet, he again returns to the project manager and notices, to his dismay, that their two floor plans are oriented differently. Once more, he starts from the beginning. It is another wasted effort, a production infirmity which, if not anticipated and controlled, may result in project disaster.

The logistics The logistics of production can be illustrated in a different way: Assume the drawing to be prepared will contain 100 different items of information, such as layouts, doors, windows, poché, and dimensions, obtained from or provided by each of four sources: project manager, architect in charge, engineer, and client. There is, then, a potential of 400 items of information to appear on the drawing.

Now, if the drafter were required to get each and every item of data needed by a separate trip to one of the four sources it would take the drafter 400 round-trips to get all the data needed to complete the drawing. Multiply those 400 trips by the number of minutes spent in collecting the data and the result is a very expensive drafting operation.

Principle of Direct Contact The example may be exaggerated, but something like it will occur unless the manager is alert to such weaknesses in drafting production. The ideal approach is to plan the work properly and provide drafting personnel with all necessary information right at the beginning. The example also illustrates the importance of achieving harmony of effort through executive ability to coordinate: the principle of direct contact. Some call it the essence of management.

Perhaps even more vital to production efficiency is the synchronizing of individual actions. Talent should be matched with tasks and responsibilities. An elementary mistake is to assign a slow drafter to complex, challenging tasks. Even worse is to deenergize ambitious talent with boring tasks.

Production planning reduces mental labor requirements to a minimum— planning what work is to be done, how it is to be done, and where, when, and by whom without always assuming everyone has the answers. While not every design professional will become, let alone want to become, a first-rate production authority, a great amount of practical know-how appears mandatory for everyone with some responsibility for securing profit for a firm.

MANAGING THE SYSTEM

The recent graduate, ready to begin a triumphant career in architecture, might not give much thought to business matters, not while a designer's career is foremost in mind. But the question has to come up sometime: "How does one become an expert manager?"

There is a unique philosophy that seems to guide successful managers, whether consciously or not: "Lazy start, panic finish." The alternative is to apply pressure on a job right at the beginning and be prepared to make best use of people, equipment, and materials. Fundamental to that correct approach is some understanding of the science of management and what it takes to be a good practitioner: the ability to win the confidence of others, display an impressive personality, manifest a determination to succeed, and guide others' thoughts toward bettering themselves.

The manager who is familiar with scientific management precepts:

- Is freed from unreliable rule-of-thumb practices
- Is freed from total dependence on instinct in the decision-making process
- Consistently applies good management technique

Scientific management implies use of analytical methods and systems such as the overlay-register technique to augment natural intuition. When a formal, scientific method has been proved, it is a serious waste not to accept it and put it to use. One example is the production of a drawing for construction purposes, the architect's graphic arts output. This is a task that is often made much more complex and time-consuming than it should be. Simplifying it is one of the prime objectives of the overlay system.

The actual technique for managing a project or a system is not nearly as well known or as perfect as it should be. Most of the time, when a project is given the go-ahead, emphasis is immediately placed on getting the drawings started without paying attention to activities that rightly precede the production effort. Proper initial preparation smooths the path of the project. Certain items of information and administrative activities are common to all projects. But because managers are often anxious to get the project off to a good start, some items will be ignored, some will be forgotten, and some will not be properly considered until the project is underway. Then they will be found to be out of sequence with the normal scheme of things and backtracking will take place. Once the manager gets involved with supervision and production, he has little time to play catch-up with overlooked administrative details.

Administrative Technique Administration is centered around the technique and tools of management. This chapter covers management technique; the following chapter covers management tools. A useful reference on the subject is Chapter 11, "Project Procedures," of the AIA *Handbook*.

Effective administration begins with Taylor's essentials of management:

- Seek better ways to do things.
- Teach people to work efficiently.
- Make cooperation the best way to achieve results.
- Delegate responsibility expertly.

The technique of managing a project has been broken down into these activities: planning, organizing, scheduling, coordinating, communicating, and directing.

Planning This decision-making activity, carried out within a specified period of time, involves strategies for the commitment of resources, people, equipment, and materials. Planning is intended to bridge the gap between here and there to achieve the best possible operating environment. People need to know purposes and objectives and have guidelines to what they are expected to accomplish. An example of planning is arranging for staff orientation on the overlay system when it is to be used for the first time. The general objective of planning is to identify and define the project elements:

- In-house line of authority and responsibility for architect-in-charge, project manager, and staff
- Production requirements, systems, and so on
- Project data, client's name, and project location and type
- Deadlines
- Parties involved: client, consultants, contractor, reproduction services
- Material provided by the client
- Special considerations: zoning and permits
- Type of construction contract
- Analysis of client's budget

Organizing Both logic and inspiration should prevail during the organizing process. The purpose of organizing is to make full use of the talent and knowledge of group members. The desired result is the team—a tightly knit group with enthusiasm and spirit. With a team it is easier to accomplish objectives than with unorganized individuals who have the same goals. "Design" is the key word; the same skills are needed for organizing as for any other form of design. The manager, as the the prime element, should be perceived as able to display authority and discretion and be unaffected by such weaknesses as discrimination and favoritism. The attitude of authority is normally commanding right at the beginning and usually lessens as team members become committed to goals and assume increasing degrees of self-direction and control.

The logical aspects of organizing are to:

- Arrange actions and functions
- Set extent of authority
- Define objectives and goals (from planning)
- Specify activities
- Adjust organization requirements as needed

The observant manager watches for individual creativity, interests, and abilities without restricting ambitions.

The activities of organizing include the following, some of which may be carried out during the planning phase:

1. Establish a project manual (Table 5-1).
2. Evaluate and summarize the design contract with the client.
3. Establish the project filing system.
4. Analyze a program if one is available.
5. Develop area and cube computations.
6. Develop or evaluate the outline specification.
7. Estimate and list drawing numbers.
8. Set up a cost control system.
9. Review the need for management tools for inclusion in the project manual.

Two excellent references for planning and organizing are AIA publications: Chapter 11, "Project Procedures," of the *Handbook*, and AIA Document D200, "Project Checklist." Both should be available during the project preparation process.

Scheduling H. L. Gantt, an associate of F. W. Taylor and a pioneer credited with over forty management principles, is the inventor of the modern scheduling device: the bar chart schedule. It has evolved into more sophisticated planning and scheduling methods such as flow process charting, critical path method (CPM), program evaluation and review technique (PERT), logical sequencing, tabular listing, and design logic. There are two general planning methods. In production planning, as with CPM and PERT, activities are grouped with or without calendar references. In detailed scheduling, as with the Gantt bar chart schedule or tabular listing, there are breakdowns of data and dates.

What type of scheduling device should the architect use? Answer that with another question, ''What's in it for me?'' The architect must try to meet a client's deadlines, but first of all he must control in-house activities that impact on profit. That always comes first.

Another planning device, of which few architects are aware, is the flow process chart. It is a graphic display of the processing activities that take place in the manufacture of a single product. However, there are architectural activities in which the device can be useful: complex reports, long-range development programs, and environmental impact statements. In those uses the chart would identify such special activities as typing, data research, conferences, printing, and correspondence. In sum, the flow process chart serves as a graphic guide to the activities in a particularly complex business operation.

The two scheduling methods that serve the architect best are the bar chart and tabular listing. Both make it much easier to keep close watch on progress. The bar chart (Figure 4-1) has a special advantage: It graphically illustrates the status of project drawings and makes it simple for a manager to quickly sense where the project stands. Drawings in trouble can be spotted at a glance. A manager should not feel a need for a time-consuming in-depth study of each and every project drawing on a routine basis. He usually has no time for that. A brief Monday morning study of the updated schedule should be enough to guide the manager's production planning for the remainder of the week. The schedule is a tool of management; it should never be a handicap. The manager should not be so overwhelmed by the tool as to be reluctant to even look at it.

Close monitoring of project status is essential for control, and that control can be made more precise by breaking the scheduling of drawings into parts. The bar for a drawing, as shown in Figure 4-1, has a four-part breakdown at 25, 50, and 75 percent completion points. Not all the parts are equal in length.

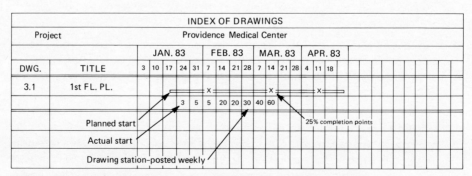

FIGURE 4-1 Bar chart schedule. It is used with main drawings only.

Different drawings will have different degrees of complexity, and there will be downtimes when a drawing is filed until it is ready to be worked on again. It is also quite important to have realistic values noted on the chart. Scheduled and actual progress should not be shown in agreement when they actually are not.

An advantage of tabular listing, often referred to as the master control index of drawings when it is used with the overlay system (Figure 4-2), is that builders can easily select from it the base sheets, overlays, or composites they need for takeoff, layout, and planning of construction activities.

Evaluating drawing status   Managers rely on experience and knowledge to judge the status of a drawing or the entire project. Usually the judgment is an intuitive exercise with or without some logic. One way to standardize judgment is to separate the elements that comprise a drawing and then assign them values that relate to the work required to place them on the drawing in their final form. For example, a floor plan might be evaluated in the following way:

	Percent
Basic layout	75
Dimensions	8
Notes	8
Title block data	2
References	2
Checking effort	5
Total	100

Evaluation is admittedly a matter of guesswork, but it improves with practice. It is the sort of task that might be delegated to other staff members for development of experience.

Coordinating   A primary management function is to harmonize individual attitudes toward reaching organization goals. To do so, management needs more than coordination; the element of cooperation is necessary. Coordinating involves differences in opinions, talents, interests, and timing—factors that are found within the team as well as outside it in the associated interests of clients, contractors, printers, and government agencies. Within the production effort,

INDEX OF DRAWINGS							
Project			Providence Medical Center				
DWG. NO.	OVER-LAY	BASE	TITLE	PLANNED START	START	% COMPL.	% COMPL.
3.1			1st. FL. PL.				
	3.1		Dimensions	3-6-83	3-12-83	40	
		a	Space Dividers	3-1-83	3-2	50	
3.2			1st. FL. CEIL. PL.				
	3.2		Grid	3-20-83	3-24	20	
		b	Space Dividers	3-1-83	3-2	50	

FIGURE 4-2   Master control index. It includes base and overlay sheets.

people need to be aware of each others' abilities and responsibilities as well as their own personal goals. One of the benefits of proper, effective organizing is that the enterprise never stays put.

Contribution Communicating and coordinating are closely related, but there is one more principle that most managers probably give little thought to. It might be called contribution. Most team members sincerely give their all for the organization's best interests, but they may fail to understand when contribution is needed. For example, a project manager might chair a meeting, emerge, compose and issue minutes of the meeting detailing action required of many of those present and then sit back and wait for feedback. And often nothing happens until he prods people. It seems to be a typical human response to be passive about volunteering information or action until it is demanded, which can be very exasperating to an impatient manager.

To coordinate effectively, the manager has to keep in mind the need to spell out the importance of contribution. Team members should volunteer actions and information without constant reminders.

Communicating Edward J. Green, a management consultant, has said that communicating may have been both the greatest technological success and the most dismal sociological failure of the twentieth century. If communicating has such potential, the implication is to emphasize the simplification of information to be provided the manager and the staff. Obviously, with the information explosion upon us, the manager has to be selective; he cannot possibly digest everything that comes his way. The best approach is one called processed data.

Communication is between manager and superior and manager and subordinate. That between manager and superior is usually restricted to intelligence or processed information passing back and forth for decision making. That between manager and subordinate is more wide open; it is less for decision making than for dealing with people problems during production. For the latter purpose the goals of communication are not always obvious.

A manager should have definite, accurate ideas of what needs to be communicated and then make certain it is understood. Complex instructions may be clearly communicated, but that does not mean they will be understood. Communicated information that is not understood is of little value. Also, the manager of communication has an influence on trust, confidence, and respect.

The following are some of the goals of communication:

- Defining work assignments
- Defining organizational goals
- Defining personal goals
- Encouraging cooperation
- Encouraging innovation
- Encouraging suggestions
- Initiating discussions about job progress and such work matters as ad-

vances in practice technique, personnel development, tardiness, absenteeism, and individual problems

The technique of communication, besides person-to-person contacts, includes charts, slide shows, newsletters, personal memos, lectures, presentations, visits to suppliers and reproduction plants, and meetings. One of management's responsibilities is the control of information to guide people in their work and enable them to make intelligent decisions. Information should be forced upon people, never held back, to encourage individual accomplishment and growth.

Directing   It was management pioneer H. L. Gantt who said, "the policy of the future will be to teach, to lead for the advantage of all." The policy of the future appears to be here, although we may not see the end of the dictatorial empire builder until that type is no longer able to produce profit from the team's efforts.

All the latest philosophy about management, however, should not be taken to mean that democratic direction consists of letting everyone decide everything. That does not work either. There is no simple alternative answer to complete removal of direction and control. Someone has to lead, direct others, and exhibit the strength that keeps the organization operating properly.

There are, essentially, three different forms of directing: autocratic, free rein, and participation. Ideal directing probably has a little of each. One of the major difficulties in decision making is to judge when decisions are within the capacities of team members once those members have been granted a voice in the process. It is worth noting certain weaknesses of two different styles. The coercive, authoritative style is useful at the organization stage, but beyond a certain point it begins to generate destructive resistance from team members. On the other hand, the free rein style can also be destructive of team goals if it is applied when the team is unprepared to accept responsibility and authority. The directing style often varies with conditions. Which style is effective depends on knowing the styles' weaknesses and strengths, and how and when to apply the strengths when they are needed.

CHAPTER FIVE

Management Tools

The modern business enterprise cannot function effectively without certain tools, and the typical architectural project, as complex as it often becomes, is no exception. Management tools are essential to successful operation, and as a rule the project manager begins assembling them as soon as the project is activated.

It is a serious mistake for anyone in top management to assume that an experienced manager is thoroughly knowledgeable about management tools or to take the position the tools are not needed at a particular time or will somehow be provided in the course of the project. Problems will be minimized by taking care to assemble most of the tools before assigning any staff to the project. All the tools of management will be needed eventually; and the sooner they are gathered, the less pressure will be encountered by the manager in the course of the work. The drafting executive may find it useful to assist the project manager and in doing so have an opportunity to judge the project manager's organization abilities. The management tools are four in number: forms control, problem solving, systems, and the project manual.

Forms Control Forms are basic management tools, and a control system should be viewed as mandatory for any office. An excellent basis for a system is supplied by the business forms produced by the American Institute of Architects and also by companies that specialize in business form preparation. Keep the system simple; only three elements are needed:

1. A three-ring binder to hold an index and samples of each form. Forms have both in-house numbers and the numbers on the forms that are obtainable from other sources such as the AIA.

2. Sample forms completed and filled in to illustrate how they are to be used. Usually these are copies of forms from actual projects. And, of course, there is the need to keep forms up to date.

3. A file cabinet to hold supplies of forms kept in separate folders.

Problem Solving   In his *Architecture by Team,* William Caudill quotes another Caudill Rowlett Scott founder, William Pena: "Only by first seeking out the problem and defining it can a valid solution be developed.... Design is problem solving;... programming is problem seeking." Problem seeking is to:

1. Establish goals
2. Collect, organize, and analyze facts
3. Uncover and test programmic concepts
4. State the *problem*

As a project undergoes development, two specific factors will influence the outcome so far as problem solving is concerned. They are identified by Caudill as *product,* the essentials of function, form, and economy, and *process,* management, design, and technology. The problem-solving procedure for business use is to:

1. Obtain a clear, concise statement of the *problem*
2. Collect facts; arrange for analysis, interpret
3. Analyze; question why, what, when, where, who, and how
4. Establish results as statements of fundamentals
5. Apply fundamentals to problems
6. Test results

All of the development activity that occurs follows such an outline.

Systems   When it comes to the architect's choice of methods of production, three basic methods are available today.

1. Traditional hand drafting
2. Overlay systems
3. Computer-aided design and drafting

As techniques are improved, architects have an ever-increasing chance of getting involved with all three methods in addition to such other productive shortcuts as scissors drafting, photodrafting, cut and paste, and appliqués.

Drafting room systems must have certain characteristics:

- They must conform to the principles of simplification and standardization.
- They must reduce or eliminate duplication of effort.

- Their objectives must be clearly defined.
- They should be simple to understand and economical to use.
- They must define the responsibilities of people.
- They must realize cost benefits.
- They must be capable of advancement to benefit users.

Among their benefits, the systems:

- Help relieve managers of routine personnel and production problems
- Facilitate stricter control of time and costs
- Provide means for constant improvement of production technique
- Encourage better management

Project Manual   The basis for good organization is the project manual (Table 5-1), which contains most of the administration guiding tools. At the end of all work the manual becomes the project history. Most tools are business forms. Those that are not and cannot be physically placed within the manual are listed and explained below. All activities of project administration are performed in conjunction with contractual and financial matters that fall within the jurisdiction of the office manager or business manager. It becomes the responsibility of the project manager to work closely with other executives of the firm to monitor all matters involving production, technical labor, expense, and contract requirements for services to the client.

A brief look at the contents of the project manual reveals how difficult the task of the manager is. Thirty or more items of project data impose a severe administrative load on the manager's personal resources of time and effort. Not all forms will be required for every project, but knowing of their existence makes it easier for the manager to be confident of selections. Since some of the forms are used during the construction phase of the project, they also are listed to make certain they are not overlooked as important administrative tools or historical records.

It should also be appreciated that some managers using some minor short-cuts for the first time will be tempted to give credit to them without realizing that they can force a manager to do more planning and organizing than before.

Other forms may be used for contract matters that concern the client, consultants, engineers, and contractors. It should be apparent that, despite the efforts of the AIA, there is still a need for standardization of forms for management use. Not all architects use all AIA forms, and not all forms designed within individual firms are known outside the firm. Consequently, there is scarcely any way to judge or compare the management techniques of members of the profession. In fact, it might be inferred that management within architecture is often viewed as a mystery, and not nearly the science it ought to be.

Keeping staff busy   Probably the most difficult management chore is keeping team members busy. Idle staff can be expensive, although downtime is often accounted for in budgets. Skilled work assignment is one way in which

TABLE 5-1 Project Manual

Form Number	Title or Description
1. AIA G807	Project Directory: listing of personnel
2. AIA G808	Project Data Form: defines scope of contract
3. AIA D200	Project Checklist: six phases of performance requirements
	General
4.	Owner's program, when available
5.	Outline specifications, when available
6.	Cost control system; usually an in-house form
	Product
7.	Program analysis; in-house form
8.	Drawing schedule; Figures 4-1 and 4-2
9.	Index of drawings
10.	Operations flowchart (overlay), Figure 5-1
11.	General notes (latest issue); copies to consultants
12.	Checklist of standard details. A team member is assigned the task of selecting details for placement on sheets; useful as a work assignment tool
13.	Abbreviations, symbols, and material indications
	Another work assignment tool; check for updating
14.	Finish schedule; developed from outline specifications
15.	Finish schedule; existing, for alteration projects
16.	Equipment schedules
17.	Special space and equipment checklist
18.	Control set. See a description at the end of this chapter; not usually included in the project manual
19.	List of program changes to determine what work is reimbursable
20.	List of drawing changes to determine what work is reimbursable
21.	Building department changes
22.	Conference report form; usually an in-house form
23. AIA G804	Register of Bid Documents
24. AIA A310	Bid Bond
25. AIA A701	Instruction to Bidders
	Construction
26.	Index of post-contract drawings (in-house)
	Services
27. AIA G712	Shop Drawing and Sample Record
28. AIA G708	Architect's Field Order
29. AIA G711	Architect's Field Report
30.	Proposal log (in-house)
31. AIA G709	Proposal Request
32.	Change order log
33. AIA G701	Change Order
34. AIA G702	Application and Certificate of Payment

gains in profit can be made; that is, by careful planning and use of effective planning tools. Two such planning tools are the sheet mock-up, sometimes referred to as a sheet model, sheet analysis, or mini-plan, and the control set of drawings.

The sheet mock-up is a layout of project data at small scale on a small sheet of paper. Usually it is drawn freehand with only a limited amount of identifying information. The sheet may be as small as 8½ by 11 in. The object is to show as accurately as possible the layout of plans and details on the final drawing. It may seem superfluous to show just one plan layout on a sheet, and one plan will usually be sufficient when the floor plans are identical. The most difficult layout sheets are for such elements as wall sections, stairs, vertical transportation, and special areas. The severest problems are associated with getting relevant information on the same sheet. Details of a penthouse just never look right when they appear on the same sheet as those of an intensive care unit.

Flow process charting   After the layout sheets are completed, a coordination or network plan is developed to show the processing plan for a series of drawings. When the overlay system is used, the project manager will need a way to control production of base sheets and overlays, as well as a way to select and order reproduction services.

In the author's view, those requirements are best met with a flow process chart such as Figure 5-1. There is no standard for such a chart, and each office usually develops its own version. As the use of the overlay system and computer-aided design expands, the need for such a form is certain to result in a commercially produced one.

Figure 5-1 is essentially a production plan that functions in the following way: One form is used for each final drawing, a composite derived from one or

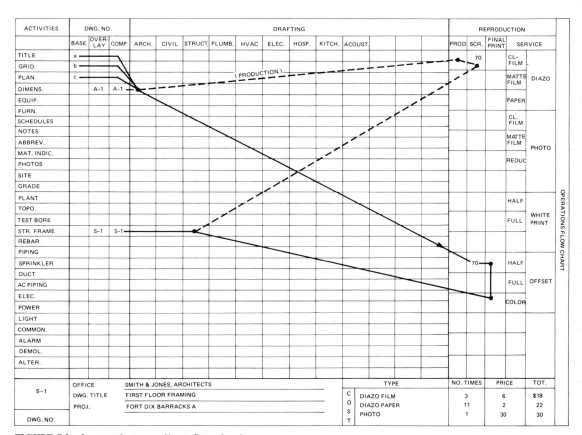

FIGURE 5-1   A sample operations flowchart.

more base sheets and overlays. (The same form can be used for other drawing sheets that do not involve the use of overlay technique.) This form provides overall, uniform planning for the entire project. The purpose of the form is to make visible and to control all production activities from drawing through reproduction services:

1. Space for architect's name, drawing title, project name
2. Final drawing number; in this example it is S-1, structural plan
3. Activities: the type of drawing to be prepared
4. Drawing numbers showing the various base sheets and overlays required to make a complete, final composite drawing for construction
5. Drafting activities
6. Reproduction services both during production and for final printing
7. Space for estimating reproduction costs

To use the form, the project manager establishes origin and destination points for the various base sheets and overlays and then connects points to show procedures. Figure 5-1 makes it simple to understand how certain sheets are used to arrive at the final drawing. A dashed line shows production processes; a solid line shows how sheets are assembled into the final version.

In the example, the First Floor Framing Plan is produced by base sheets:

a Title block

b Framing grid

c Floor plan

A-1 Dimension overlay

These sheets are then routed to reproduction with an order specifying a 70 percent screen on the diazo reproduction the structural engineer is to use as a background for preparation of overlay S-1, Framing Plan. The same reproduction services would be used in development of the composite for the final working drawing S-1.

Figure 5-2 is an example of a form that can lessen mental burdens during the course of a project. The flowchart is for a particularly complex project in which a large number of individually designed and separately built doctor's offices are to be included in an existing or recently completed building. The manager must keep track of fifteen suites each of which involves fifteen separate procedures. By recording all the procedures on one sheet, the manager can easily keep sight of the 225 procedures and so go a long way toward keeping the project under strict control.

The chart can be made more complex by adding personnel names and dates, but it should contain no more data than necessary to do what is expected of it. Managers have a tendency to disregard tools that take too much time to administer.

Planning takes time and effort that may not always be budgeted. It is easy for top management to get anxious about planning efforts that do not appear to

PRODUCTION PROCEDURES						INDIVIDUAL PROJECTS							Rockville Doctor's Office Building				
Suite	Tenant Dr.	Plan	Title	Date	Plan	Casework	Ceil.	Plumbing	HVAC	Light	Power	Tel.	Fire Safe.	Permit	Inspec.	Occup.	
101	A	→	→	→	→	→	→		→			→	→				
102	B	→															
103	C	→	→	→													
104	D	→	→	→	→	→	→	→	→	→	→	→	→	→			
201	A																
202	B	→	→	→	→		→	→									
203	C																
204	D	→	→		→												
205	E																
301	A	→															
302	B																
303	C																
401	A																
402	B																
501	A																

FIGURE 5-2 Flowchart of a particularly complex project.

be accomplishing anything, but planning is an important management responsibility that facilitates the activation of a project and the use of people.

Control set The project set of drawings can be used in conjunction with other planning tools. It has unique flexibility as a work assignment device; it can be interrupted during preparation and before completion in order to identify production work that can be assigned to drafting personnel who may be available before actual schedule starting time. It is usually a complete set of schematics or preliminary drawings, although normally at smaller scale than the final working drawings. Usually the drawings will be the schematics of the project, and they should be identical with the drawings approved by the client.

If the manager is new to the project, the first step is a careful review of the drawings and outline specifications. Once work gets underway, it becomes more and more difficult to backtrack to catch up with overlooked or neglected data.

Schematics and Design Development At this point it is worth reviewing two well-known terms: "schematics" and "design development." Both terms are defined in Chapter 11, "Project Procedures," of the AIA *Handbook,* but possibly not as clearly as some architects would like. It appears that some architects ignore the design development phase of construction documents and proceed right from schematics to working drawings, as used to be done years ago. In Chapter 11 of the *Handbook,* the point is made that design development serves as a cautionary stopping point for work to confirm that, although the client may not understand what the term means, essential, basic project features, when delineated at final scale and in more detail, are actually what the client will accept for second-stage approval in writing. (The first-stage approval is schematics.)

Again quoting Chapter 11, "Design development documents, when approved, may form the basis for construction documents." It would, then, be normal practice to produce design development drawings primarily as the initial stage of working drawings and to extend them during the working drawing phase as complete drawings for construction. In work assignment planning, design development is an interruption point in drawing production. The sooner the client's approval is obtained, the sooner the project can get back into production.

Planning Work For work assignment planning, the control set is used as follows:

1. Each schematic drawing is marked in crayon or colored ink to block out, by circling or marking with section arrows, elements and features to be placed on final sheets: plans, elevations, vertical transportation, and so on.

2. A review of the outline specifications also takes place, and notes regarding methods, materials, and products are added to the set.

3. After all sheets of the control set are color-marked, a system of numbering is begun. Numbers are placed on each individual sheet to identify

elements, such as plans, wall sections, and vertical transportation, to be drawn on final sheets.

4. The drawing index can then be started by assigning numbers to existing base sheets and overlays and estimating all other sheets needed for the project.

5. As an alternative, a sheet can start with a sketch number to expedite identification and control. A sketch number need not identify a full sheet; it can identify just a detail or an element that can later be combined with other sketch number elements for placement on a full-size sheet. The numbering method can be quite simple. In a large project, floor plans might be numbered in the SK-100 series, elevations in the SK-200 series, and so on. Sketch numbering systems are quick, imprecise, and temporary; the system naturally vanishes during progress of the job.

6. The marked-up control set then serves as an index of sketches, since there is no need for a formal list.

7. The marked-up control set will probably identify details that should be studied briefly to determine if they need further work for inclusion in the final group of working drawings. This helps make sure that certain important but difficult-to-detect details are not overlooked.

8. The sheet mock-up can then be started. As soon as sheets are made up, the project manager can schedule drafting help.

9. There are cautions to be observed during the design development phase. That work is not started on elements and details that are appropriate for the working drawing phase.

10. As people are put to work as drawings get underway, elements and project features that are being worked on are marked in color on the control set. The marking begins to provide graphic picturization of the status of the project, a clear picture to use for reporting progress to superiors.

11. The combination of the control set and the sheet mock-up enables team members to select work assignments during any absence of the manager so the project will move along smoothly.

12. Another feature of the sketch-numbering technique is to add a letter suffix—SK-25E, for example—whenever a sheet is worked on or changed for reason of client's wishes, consultant conflicts, or careless drafting. The suffix becomes a quality control measure because it indicates when a problem is being caused by personnel, the client, or construction complexities.

With the project control set, the manager can easily visualize progress as well as be alerted whenever production problems develop.

CHAPTER SIX

System Components and Equipment

This chapter covers the component requirements for three basic functions: system operations, drafting, and reproduction services. Photographic quality for the final architectural product is a primary purpose of the overlay system. Photography does not dominate the system, however, because not all the reproduction services rely on it. In this important respect the system differs from the earlier overlay-register techniques, which were heavily dependent on in-house investment in photographic equipment and trained personnel. Today, the architect can provide some of the necessary equipment and knowledge and rely confidently on the reprographic part of the team to provide the know-how, well-trained and experienced personnel, and sophisticated equipment that are needed to support the design effort. That is true no matter what the size of the project or the design firm using the system.

Components, equipment, and system methods have been proved, so new users of the system can profit from the investment and experience of far-sighted leaders and need not reinvent the wheel. There are, however, certain to be improvements as the system is put to greater use.

SYSTEM COMPONENTS

The basic components of the overlay system are registration bars, punches, polyester sheet film, equipment, and services.

Registration Bars Since proper registration of several drawing sheets is critical to both accuracy and productivity, the registry method must be precise, positive, and convenient to use by all the people involved in drafting and reproduction. The established method depends on registration bars and matching punching devices, both of which are commercially available.

Registration bars are thin strips of stainless steel approximately 27 in long and 1 in wide. On a bar seven metal pins of ¼-in diameter are usually mounted. Each pin is ¼ in high, and the pins are equally spaced along the bar. Bars with different lengths and heights can also be obtained, but the pin spacing is standard. A nine-pin registration bar, for example, adds some precision, although the seven-pin bar is commonly used.

Mounting a registration bar on a drafting board is simply a matter of taping it to the board. Once mounted on the pins, the base and overlays also are taped down, but only to keep them from pulling off the pins during drafting procedures. Basically it is the registration bar on the drafting board that holds the sheets in alignment and registration while drafting progresses.

Registration bars of the same type are mounted on reprographic equipment, contact printers, copyboards, negative holders, and offset printing presses when running black and white or color. Commonly called pin bars, they ensure continuity of registration during all production processes from drafting board to contact printer, copyboard, camera, projector, and press.

Punches Since a seven-pin bar is standard for overlay system use, a matching punching device must be available to punch sheets of material for both drafting and reproduction purposes. The punch, which is similar to the small office punch for three-ring-binder holes, is a sizable investment, and it will usually be available at the reproduction plant. To assure accuracy, the machine is made with a narrow throat so it can accept only a few sheets of material at a time. The normal practice is to punch sheets individually.

Note: It cannot be overemphasized that successful use of the overlay system depends on following standard registry procedures. Cross hairs, targets, and individual registry pins are inadvisable. A fundamental purpose of any efficiency device is to solve management problems, not create them. Overlay-register techniques work, and they will benefit users to the extent that standard registration methods are used. Other methods are likely to cause production confusion and delays and unnecessary expense and lead to unsatisfactory results. The serious problems created by imprecise punching and registration through the use of targets are aggravated by sheet slippage and eye-balled misregistration during reproduction as well as drafting.

Polyester Sheet Film Getting good registration through the use of pin bars is one thing, but holding it throughout the production of the end product is another. Sheet registration will suffer and results will be unsatisfactory unless a proper sheet material is used.

The sheet material that has made the overlay-register technique successful in architecture is a stable-base polyester film used for both drafting and reproduction. The film has outstanding characteristics. Chemically known as polyethylene terephthalate, it is a polymer that was discovered in 1941 in the United Kingdom. By modern technological manufacturing processes, it is now converted into continuous webs of various thicknesses. Polyester film serves overlay system purposes well because of its exceptionally high transparency, great strength, flexibility, and dimensional stability. The material is long-lived, extremely durable, and inert to most solvents. It does not discolor with age, and it provides sharp, clear prints of superior quality. At the drafting board, it is easy to work on, takes ink and pencil readily, and erases quickly and cleanly. In those respects alone, the material makes a significant contribution to drafting productivity.

When used with overlay-register technique, all drafting film and reproduction film is punched along the top edge of the sheet with seven holes to correspond to the seven pins of the registry pin bar. Before using drafting film or photo film, sheets that are cut recently from roll stock should be stored flat for at least 48 hr to minimize size changes in the material.

Three types of polyester film are needed by the overlay system: drafting film, sensitized-silver photographic film, and diazo film, which is developed by humidified ammonia vapors in whiteprinters. The silver photo sheet material is about ten times costlier than the diazo material.

Drafting film is available in rolls and sheets of various drafting sizes. It has a factory-applied nonfibrous matte drafting surface that makes possible a dense, uniform line with less pressure and ink dispersion. Most matte surface sheets are made with an antistatic treatment to prevent the problems that occur when sheets are filed together: the film sticking to a printing cylinder or separation of surface and backing prior to development. Those problems could cause damage to the original drawing and perhaps to the reproduction machine. The matte surface is of three types: one for pencil, one for pen and ink, and one for either pencil or ink.

Pencils Three kinds of pencil are suitable for use on polyester film: graphite, plastic, and a combination of the two. Graphite leads are best restricted to soft grades such as H and F. Very hard leads must be avoided; for if they are used and heavy pressure is applied to get a dark line, the lead will groove the film. The grooves may not be removable, and they could cause ghost images to emerge when the sheet is printed. Plastic leads have a softer, crayon-like feel when drafting, and lines drawn with them are more smear-resistant than those drawn with graphite leads. The combination graphite and plastic lead causes less smear on the film and will wear longer than any graphite lead.

Note: When drafting on film, it is inadvisable to mix drafting materials. Pencil and ink will produce definite differences in line density that may not be evident while drafting but are likely to be obvious on reproductions.

Pen and ink Ink drafting is increasing in popularity partly because of the excellent surface qualities of drafting film and partly because of computer output plotting requirements. Drafting ink produces superior, uniform lines, but not without problems that are centered around viscosity and climatic conditions. The darkest lines are obtained with the thickest ink, which is also slow to dry. Quicker-drying inks are less opaque, but the quality difference is minor. Some inks may work well in humid areas but not so well in arid ones. Manufacturers offer a variety of products to suit different areas of use.

Three pen points are used: stainless steel, jewel, and tungsten carbide. Stainless-steel pen points wear out extremely fast on the matte surface of drafting film; the other two types last over ten times longer. Jewel points are popular for drafting; the tungsten carbide points were developed primarily for computer plotting purposes.

Erasing drafting film Pencil lines are faster and easier to remove from drafting film than from paper, vellum, or even the little-used linen. When lines are to be erased from drafting film, certain precautions must be observed. Damage to the matte surface of the film must be avoided. The damage may be caused by grooving the surface with excessive drafting pressure on hard leads. Also, heavy pressure when using hard erasers is likely to remove the matte surface and make it almost impossible to draw a line back on that particular spot on the film. A nonabrasive soft vinyl or plastic eraser works well for removing pencil lines and will not damage the surface.

There are a number of ways to remove ink lines from drafting film. Some inks may come off easily with a wet sponge or cloth; other inks can be removed with a soft vinyl eraser. Large ink-drafted areas can be erased with a sponge or soft cloth dampened with alcohol or a glass-cleaning solution. To remove indelible ink, a special eraser or a special fluid in combination with a vinyl eraser is needed.

Photographic Reproduction Film Sheet materials for use at a reproduction facility are of two types: photographic and diazo. Photographic film is available in sheets and rolls. Basically, it is the same as drafting film except that it is coated with a silver process-sensitized emulsion on either a previously applied matte surface or the smooth film. The unexposed emulsion coating is removed from the film after exposure by either hand or automatic chemical processing. After developing and processing, the sheet will then have remaining on it both a photographic image and a matte drafting surface if the sheet was made with it.

There are two types of photosensitive reproduction film. One produces a moist-erasable and the other a fixed, or hard-line, image. Moist-erasable film is also referred to in the industry as wash-off film. Both types produce dense, black, ink-like lines and images of outstanding quality for sharp, clear, readable printing.

Photographic film is of three types: matte on one side, and smooth on the other; matte on both sides, and no matte surface on either side of the sheet.

Erasing reproduction film Images and lines can be removed from moist-erasable, or wash-off film with just a moistened rubber eraser. The lines and images are quite durable, and water alone will not cause any damage to either the lines or the matte surface. Some rubbing action is necessary to effect removal of lines and images. Hand-drafted pencil or ink lines and also photographic lines can be removed and corrections easily made with either ink or pencil. There is no loss of line quality.

For removal of lines and images from fixed, or hard-line, photoreproductions, treatment with a two-part chemical solution is needed. One chemical has a dissolving action; the other neutralizes the first. Some time is lost while waiting for the chemicals to dry before the sheet can be thoroughly rinsed with a wet cloth or sponge to remove all traces of the two chemicals. Then the sheet must be dried thoroughly before any corrections can be made. The main advantage of the fixed, hard-line photoreproduction is the durability of lines and images, which is somewhat better than that on moist-erasable film.

Photographic reproductions are used in the drawing production process (1) for making copies of base sheets, (2) as intermediates, and (3) for final compositing of base and overlay sheets.

Diazo Materials Diazo reproduction film has an important part in controlling costs and achieving economies for the overlay system. Like both drafting and photographic film, it is polyester sheet material with a matte surface on either one or both sides. On one side is a factory-applied sensitized coating that, after exposure, is changed by ammonia processing to leave lines and images on the sheet. The color of the lines and images can be blue, brown, or black at the option of the architect or the repro plant.

Although all diazo products are cost-beneficial for the overlay system, the potential uses are somewhat confusing because of the many terms applied to the material: brown lines, sepia transparencies, diazo intermediates, second originals, and duplicate originals. And not all the terms refer to polyester film products. Generally, there are three uses for diazo products, two of which are not directly related to overlay-register processes:

1. Second originals or copies, as substitutes for original working drawing tracings to save wear and tear on the originals when a large quantity of whiteprinting must be done. These diazo prints can be on paper.

2. For shipping long distance to suppliers and subcontractors, who then get printing done locally. Again, the diazo second original can be obtained on paper.

Primary use Diazo products are primarily used in the overlay system to make copies of base sheets and for check printing. To make a copy of a base sheet for a floor plan for an engineer or consultant, for example, a diazo copy of the base sheet, previously punched for registry, is placed on the drafting board and pinned to a taped-down seven-pin registration bar. For a hand-drafting overlay, a punched sheet of drafting film is then placed over the base sheet and pinned and taped to the pin bar. All data drafted on the overlay sheet will be perfectly registered and aligned with data on the base or background sheet.

After hand drafting of all complementary data on the overlay is complete, the diazo reference copy may be discarded, since it will have no further use. The only base sheet to be preserved is the original. From a practical standpoint, however, the diazo film copy remains valid until either all drawing is complete and there is no further use for it or the base sheet is significantly changed. If the latter is true, the usual technique is to issue another diazo copy (another throwaway) so thc cngineers and consultants can change their own design data on the overlays they have created without their having to make any floor plan changes.

All final compositing processes make use of the original base sheet and original overlay tracings (not diazo copies), which are retained as permanent file copies. The final composite can be either a diazo film or a photoreproduction film, whichever is required.

When diazo material is to be used for check printing of individual drawings or for volume printing, individual sheets are produced by compositing the base sheet and one or more overlays. The resulting diazo, which can be either film or paper, is usually called a second original. Diazo film for reproduction of base sheets for use by engineers and consultants in overlay development is usually smooth on both sides. The material has a little better clarity than that with a matte surface. The sensitized coating is factory-applied directly to the clear base of the film. Some refer to this material as throwaway.

Properties and thicknesses Diazo polyester film and vellum are available with a variety of image lines. One type of diazo reproduction has a nonerasable line; another has a line that can be eradicated with a special solution; a third has a line that can be removed with a moistened medium-coarse eraser. Nonerasable diazo reproductions are also nondraftable. Made on smooth film, they are usually base sheet copies of floor plans, so unauthorized changes can not be made on them. They are the throwaways. Another useful diazo product is adhesive-backed sensitized film that can be used for scissors drafting and appliqué shortcuts.

Diazo film is available in 2-,3-,5-, and 7-mil thicknesses. Some attention should be given to film properties in order to take full advantage of lower-priced products. Films that are at least 3 mils thick are required for pin bar drafting, but reproducible composites on 2-mil film or vellum will be less expensive for printing large quantities of prints for checking or progress review.

Note: Although they are important production materials, diazo products have the disadvantage of deteriorating over a period of time. They may not have sufficient archival quality for long-term filing. Usually a diazo film sheet, which might be the final original tracing for construction purposes, will be reproduced for filing purposes. Acceptable processes include full-size reproduction by photography or large-size copier or reduction to an 8½- by 11-in negative. When drafting production is complete, original diazo materials may be discarded, although it is good practice to review their value for use by subcontractors and suppliers during the planning and construction phases of a project.

DRAFTING ROOM COMPONENTS AND EQUIPMENT

The primary investment might be limited to registration bars, polyester drafting film, and a stock of pencils, pens, pen holders, ink, and erasers. The purchase or rental of reproduction equipment is also recommended. Basic equipment requirements are a whiteprinter and a flatbed vacuum frame printer often called a platemaker.

Figure 6-1 is the plan of a well-equipped, modern in-house reproduction facility appropriate for almost any architectural firm. The investment in space and equipment offers a return of long-range, consistent benefits to the firms willing to make the commitment. This recommendation is not intended to minimize or downgrade the importance of commercial services. The mix of in-house and commercial services is a practical matter. For example, it is not good practice to interrupt normal production continuity to get out-of-house printing no matter how fast the printing can be done. Progressive reprographics firms are realizing that and are providing lease-purchase arrangements and personnel training and/or personnel support to make it easier for architects to acquire first-class reproduction facilities. This is a much more realistic approach to the architect's acquisition of modern production technology.

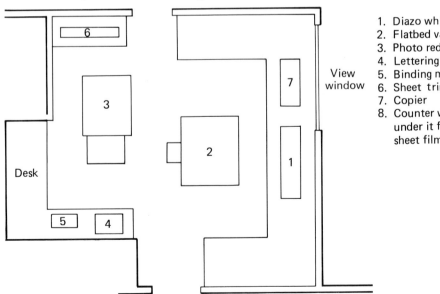

1. Diazo whiteprinter
2. Flatbed vacuum frame
3. Photo reduction (A.B. Dick)
4. Lettering machine
5. Binding machine
6. Sheet trimmer
7. Copier
8. Counter with flat files under it for paper and sheet film storage

FIGURE 6-1 Plan of a modern in-house reproduction facility. (Cohen-Karydas and Associates, Chartered, Washington, D.C.)

Diazo Whiteprinter   The diazo whiteprinter (Figure 6-2) is available as either a floor-standing model or a countertop unit. It replaces the blueprint machine, of which there are few to be seen anymore. The whiteprint it produces, from an original tracing, can be either a blue or a black line on a white background at the architect's option. This copy is produced in two stages: first the image of the original is transferred to a sensitized coating on paper or film and then, by a second run through the ammonia developer section, an exact copy of the original is produced. The whiteprinter thereby has dual use: It not only produces a whiteprint but also serves as the developer for material exposed on a flatbed printer. It may also be used to produce composited copies of base sheets and overlays, but it is not ideal for that use. The machine operates by a roller action that causes drawings to get out of registration. The flatbed printer is better suited to composite production.

Flatbed Vacuum Frame Printer   The flatbed vacuum frame printer, or platemaker, shown in Figure 6-3 is an effective element in drafting production and general reprographics work as well as the overlay system. It is used primarily to produce backgrounds, copies of base sheets, and composites. That is why, although originally marketed as a printer's platemaker, the flatbed printer has been found so valuable in the drafting room.

To expose an original to sensitized material, either paper or polyester film, the printer uses powered vacuum within a leakproof enclosure to hold the sheets together. There are two types of vacuum frames: the usual flatbed and a

FIGURE 6-2   A whiteprinter. (Ozalid Corporation)

unique type called a flip-top. The latter speeds up production somewhat by feeding from both sides; while material on one side is being exposed, the other side can be loaded.

Equipment makers differ on the number of sheets in a sandwich that will produce a legible composite drawing. When compositing is being done, the sandwich of sheets is so arranged that the sheet with the greatest amount of data is nearest the sensitized emulsion coating on the film sheet. For example, the floor plan may be considered background data and so will be placed farthest away from the emulsion side of the sheet. The result will give the floor plan a subdued appearance like that obtained by screening, a process described in Chapter 3.

The sheets within the vacuum frame will be held flat and tight together in registration on a pin bar while being exposed to light. The light sources in vacuum frames differ. Commercial equipment has a high-intensity light from a point source for fast exposures that produce sharp prints. The tight light seals with which this equipment is provided also prevent air leakage while vacuum is being produced. Some flatbed printers can double as light tables.

For overlay compositing purposes, the difference between flatbed and reprographic printing is the technique. In the diazo process, all sheets have to be exposed at the same time. In process camera-projector production, the sheets in a sandwich are projected back individually via reduction negatives onto a single sheet of sensitized polyester film mounted on a vertical copyboard. The reproductions are sharp and of high quality, and in theory any number of sheets can be combined. In diazo reproduction, the manufacturers suggest a limit of five sheets, although that might be considered the practical limit of photography as well.

FIGURE 6-3   A flatbed vacuum printer. (Ozalid Corporation)

THE REPROGRAPHIC FACILITY

Even the architect with some in-house reproduction capability will need the services of a reprographics facility, and the more the architect becomes involved with the overlay system, the more valuable the reprographic professional will become. The services that the latter can provide include photographic reproduction work and volume printing for check and progress review and bidding and construction purposes. That being so, it is decidedly in the best interests of the design professional to become knowledgeable about the reprographics industry and its services, equipment, and materials. Reprographic plant layout will differ from one facility to another, so the following description is only a brief introduction.

Communication between the reprographics plant and the architect is the first problem to arise; it starts with orders for services and materials involving the overlay system. It is not easy at first to clearly spell out exactly what services and products are needed, and that is why a number of ideas about order forms have been offered. The operations flowchart (Figure 5-1) can be submitted along with the reprographics firm's own order form to help avoid misunderstanding about what is ordered.

Plant Layout   The reprographics firm will employ the same basic components as the architect but with emphasis on registration bars, polyester reproduction film, and industrial equipment. The equipment and arrangement of a typical reprographics facility are diagrammed in Figure 6-4, which shows the movement of material submitted by the design firm and that furnished by the reprographics firm. An H arrangement is shown in the diagram, but the same flow is possible in either an L or a straight-line layout.

Processing overlay system orders within the production department is a specialized function more suited to a process-line layout than a product layout. In a process line, process is intermittent and work is completed in distinctly separated workstations. Some of the advantages of the process layout are the following:

- There is enough flexibility to run both overlay system orders and custom photography orders.
- Schedules can easily be adjusted to cope with most order problems and equipment malfunctions.
- Supervision is more effective.

Equipment   The items discussed are essential for overlay system production. Not all equipment, services, and procedures provided at reprographic plants are covered.

Register punches   The register punch is not usually found in an architect's office because it is relatively expensive. Also, a certain amount of floor space is required for the punch itself and for storing sheet film of both the photographic and the diazo type. Punches are commonly activated by hand, but power-activated punches also are available for faster production. A recent development is the nine-pin registration system of pin bars and punches that may eventually become standard.

Punches are made with only backstops and not with side stops, so it is normal to have pin holes line up even though the edges of sheets will not be in perfect alignment. However, some care must be taken, when punching and when selecting a sheet to be placed on a pin bar, that edges are not too far out of alignment. For example, a badly punched overlay sheet may not have enough room left along its side or an edge for the overlay identification number that is to appear in the title block.

Two register punches are usually to be found in most reprographics plants. One is located in the photographic exposure room and another in the materials-handling room. The latter is used for sheets that do not have light-sensitive coatings. Duplication of punches assures the safety of light-sensitive materials and avoids disruption of darkroom activities. The storage facilities for sheet materials are countertop-height filing cabinets. They are flat-drawer types whose tops make them convenient work spaces for the punches.

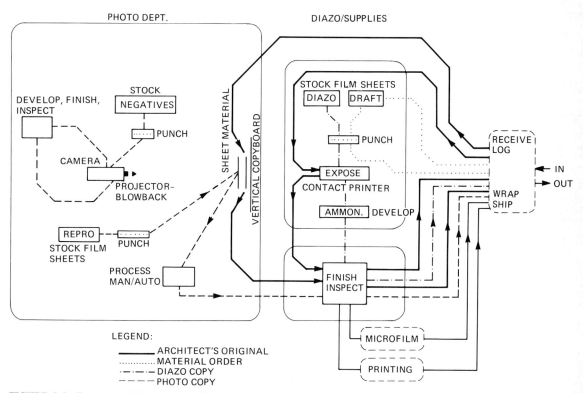

FIGURE 6-4 Reprographic services flowchart.

Contact printers Contact printing equipment for both diazo and photo film will usually be commercial versions of the flatbed and flip-top vacuum units. They are set horizontally, and another type is set vertically. The three operate in the same way so far as exposing and developing are concerned.

PHOTOGRAPHIC PRODUCTION

Modern photographic technology has endowed overlay-register techniques with far greater versatility and quality than were possible with the Corps of Engineers overlay-composite method. The latter was limited to full-size contact photography. Today the camera and projector are combined in one unit that can produce 8½- by 11-in negatives, although more sophisticated units can produce negatives of up to 21- by 28- in size for mammoth projects. The 8½- by 11-in size is more commonly used, however. The smaller negatives, called reduction negatives or repro formats, have important advantages of which the design professional should be aware:

- They are easier to handle, register, and place in the camera-projector unit.
- They require far less time to produce and cost less to work on. The work needed might be blocking out, or opaquing, unwanted data, particularly for restoration work.
- They cost much less than full-size negatives used in contact photography.
- They are easier and less expensive to file.
- They provide important options: scale changing and multiple negative projection such as screen, base sheet, and overlay reproduction—all with precise accuracy and excellent quality.

Camera-Projector Unit Various designs of camera-projectors are available; they include overhead track-mounted units (Figures 6-5 and 6-6), floor-track-mounted units, bed-mounted units, and fixed-focus units that are fixed in position. All these units rely on vacuum to hold film materials perfectly flat and free of distortion during exposure and projection.

Projection Technique An important production use of the camera-projector, centered around the reduction negative, is to make photographic composites of base overlay sheets with or without screening any images. This special technique, known as multiple negative projection, is accomplished as follows:

1. A punched sheet of 8½- by 11-in negative film is placed on three pins in the camera film holder.

2. A drawing received from the architect—a base sheet or overlay sheet that is to be part of the composite, previously punched for registration—is attached directly to pins on the vertical copyboard in front of the camera-projector unit.

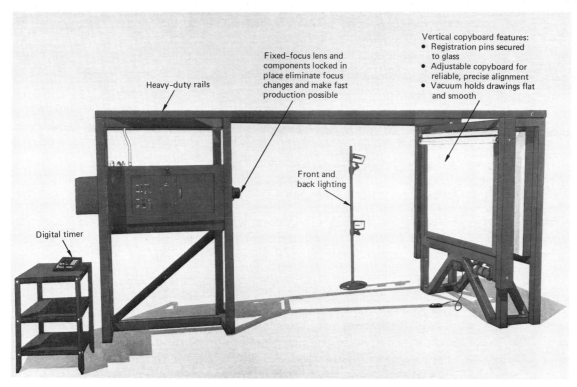

Heavy-duty rails

Fixed-focus lens and components locked in place eliminate focus changes and make fast production possible

Vertical copyboard features:
• Registration pins secured to glass
• Adjustable copyboard for reliable, precise alignment
• Vacuum holds drawings flat and smooth

Front and back lighting

Digital timer

FIGURE 6-5 Fixed-ratio camera-projector. (Data Optics, Inc.)

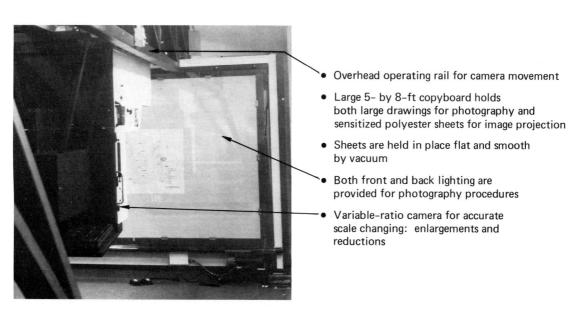

• Overhead operating rail for camera movement

• Large 5- by 8-ft copyboard holds both large drawings for photography and sensitized polyester sheets for image projection

• Sheets are held in place flat and smooth by vacuum

• Both front and back lighting are provided for photography procedures

• Variable-ratio camera for accurate scale changing: enlargements and reductions

FIGURE 6-6 Variable-ratio camera-projector. (Data Optics, Inc.)

Early-model copyboards had to have a registration bar taped to the copyboard to hold sheets of material.

3. The original drawing on the copyboard is exposed to light, and the image is recorded on the reduction negative. The negative is then removed from the film holder, developed, and inspected for quality.

4. After the negative is approved, the drawing on the copyboard is removed, another original drawing is mounted in its place, a new negative is placed in the film holder of the camera unit, and another photograph is taken.

The photographic procedure is repeated until all the drawings that are to make up the composite have been recorded on negatives. Then comes the projection portion of the procedure:

1. An approved negative of one of the original sheets is placed back in the camera film holder (now the projector).

2. A sheet of photosensitive polyester film is taken from stock, punched, and placed in position on a pin bar of the copyboard.

3. The projector light is turned on for a predetermined period of time and the negative image is projected on the sheet of sensitized film. With this technique, called the burn and double burn, it makes no difference in what order the negatives of originals are projected back onto the one sheet that will become the composite, except when one sheet or more is to be screened. That negative is projected through a full-size screen on polyester film placed on top of the sheet on the copyboard. The screen might be punched for positioning, or, since no registry is involved, just be taped to the board. (Screening is discussed below.)

4. When the projector light has turned off, the negative is removed, another negative is placed in the film holder, and the projector light is turned on again to project still another film that is "burned" onto the sheet of film on the copyboard.

Steps 1 to 4 are repeated until all the negatives have been projected back onto the sheet of film. The sheet is then removed from the copyboard and run through an automatic processor, if one is available, and checked for quality. It may require opaque corrections, and it may even have to be redone. The quality-approved product is a composite drawing, usually on a draftable matte surface, with the appearance of hand-drafting and the quality of a photograph. Individual base and overlay sheet negatives of the composite are then filed.

Screens One of the most complex subjects confronting a design professional using photographic services is the production of something variously called phantom image, shadow print, ghost image, and subordinate image. Whatever it is called, it is produced by screening. A screen is a sheet of film bearing a pattern of lines or dots of various sizes. There are three types of pattern: standard screen values, bi-angle tints, and line tints. All three have established values that indicate the amount of line that will remain on the reproduction. The effect of the screen is to make a line gray rather than black.

Contact screens are made from glass masters and reproduced onto polyester film. To make a screen master, a sheet of glass polished perfectly flat is coated with a material resistant to hydrofluoric acid. A diamond cutter on an automatic ruling machine scribes lines through the coating and into the glass in accordance with screen design. After it is scribed, the glass is immersed in hydrofluoric acid solution, which etches the scribed lines. When etching is complete, the coating is removed and the etched areas are filled with an opaque material. For cross-line screens, two pieces of glass are scribed and then cemented together so the lines are perpendicular to each other. The transfer to polyester film is then made by the usual photographic processes.

Screening has important influences on drawing quality, and the architect is advised to work out screening requirements with a reprographics specialist. It is always good practice to have a sample print of a screened reproduction made before volume printing, full or half size, is ordered.

Film Processing Most plants will have both manual and automatic film-processing capability. Automatic processors are self-contained, high-speed production machines that both process and quick-dry sheets of film and paper after exposure in contact printers or camera-projector units. Processing a large sheet of material, a typical architectural drawing, takes an automatic machine about 90 sec. Developing, fixing, washing, and drying are combined in a single, continuous operation.

The manual processing of exposed film requires large developing sinks and air drying, and it is a slow, time-consuming operation. But although automatic processing is preferable from a production standpoint, manual processing is often preferred for quality work. Also it is needed as a backup when the automatic processor is down for maintenance or repair. Darkrooms for processing small-size negatives are equipped with conventional sinks, dryers, and automatic processors.

Finish Room The finish room is usually located near the wrapping and shipping area; in it reproductions are inspected, trimmed, and assembled for shipping. Here also small-size negatives will often be worked on, as for opaquing out unwanted data. It must therefore have light tables and materials and equipment for working negatives. Ammonia-developing equipment will be needed for processing diazo film and paper. Diazo printers are usually employed for the purpose, and contact printers are located nearby to maintain smooth production flow.

A finish room must have a dust-, humidity-, and temperature-controlled environment and be well lighted, since the work performed in it—evaluating the quality of production material—requires intense concentration. Comfortable working conditions are therefore given high priority.

Printing Low-cost multicolor offset printing is one of the important benefits of the overlay system. Now, in addition to long-established blueprint, white-print, and black-and-white offset print, the architect has the capacity to publish construction documents in color. That is because color offset printing is achieved through the technique of color separation. Normally that is an expensive manual procedure performed at the printing plant. But with the overlay system, the color separation is available through the usual process of drafting base sheets and overlays and at far less cost. Individual base sheets and overlays can be offset-printed in different colors.

When color offset printing has been selected by the design professional, the technical procedure is to make a registered printing press plate for each base and overlay, as well as for any drawing that was drafted complete without use of a base or overlay technique.

The multiple-negative projection technique described earlier in this chapter is also used to produce half-size printing plates. Offset printing in half size will usually also involve black and white when drawings have been created without base sheets and overlays. The next question facing the architect is how to get full-size prints—temporary second originals—for building permits, checking, and review. The options include:

1. Diazo paper reproduction

2. Diazo polyester film reproductions

3. Full-size contact photographic reproductions

4. Full-size process camera-projector reproductions made from the negatives needed to make the printing plate

The choice depends on in-house reproduction facilities, the numbers of copies needed, and the cost estimates provided by the reproduction facility. Volume color printing is cost-competitive with volume whiteprinting for construction purposes. The practical minimum is about 100 copies, which is a significant output for any design firm.

The overlay system presents a unique opportunity for the progressive designer to show growth as a professional, particularly when cover sheets for construction documents and specifications are concerned. The field of creative expression is wide open. Dramatic, colorful, attention-getting cover sheets can be created through the combination of the overlay system and photodrafting. Together they provide the architect with impressive new tools for business promotion purposes.

CHAPTER SEVEN

Production

Data separation, a unique principle of the overlay system, has to do with base sheets, overlays, and composites. They are the fundamentals of the overlay-register drafting technique.

ESSENTIALS

Essential to the production of base sheets, overlays, and composites are the polyester film and metal registration bars introduced in Chapter 6. As we said there, polyester film is the only sheet material with the proper characteristics for use with the system. It is stable dimensionally, and it is strong, flexible, and almost impossible to tear. Care in handling it is necessary, however, to prevent stretching it, because it is subject to permanent deformation. And although the film is quite flexible, its proper attitude for production purposes is flat to avoid stretching. Folds in the film create serious crease defects that not only collect dirt but, if deep enough, may prevent tight, flat contact during drafting and production.

Polyester Film Selection Polyester film is manufactured by a number of companies, and the various brands have similar characteristics. The differences between them can be detected only by experts. Choice by the architect is largely dependent on availability in the particular area and any private product testing that may have been carried out.

   As sheets are handled during production and reproduction, the registry holes punched in them are subjected to considerable wear. That is one reason why film of at least 4-mil thickness should be used for drafting and most reproduction purposes. Film thicker than 4 mils tends to reduce the clarity of image lines in composite reproductions. A 3-mil film, which is about half as strong as 4-mil film, is more likely to suffer deformation from stretching and serious wear at pin holes that can adversely affect the precise registry of sheets that is mandatory for the overlay system. Otherwise, 3-mil sheets, which, of course, cost less, are satisfactory for other steps in the production process. Table 7-1 is a complete guide to production sheet materials—drafting film, photosensitive film, and diazo sensitized film and vellum.

Registry   The second essential to data separation is the registry system. Information on a particular project element, such as an architectural floor plan, is placed on different sheets. It must not only be accurately placed on any one sheet but also be precisely related to the information on all the related sheets. In early registry systems cross hairs or targets were used for aligning one sheet over another, but the method was slow, inaccurate, error-prone, and suitable only for rough work. Even when taped or stapled together, sheets are subject to slippage. In another early method two or more individual register pins were taped to a surface and used to hold two sheets taped or stapled together. That also produced unsatisfactory results.

The necessary positive registry system is centered around the registration bar described in Chapter 6. Its seven round brass pins are spaced 4¼ in on center. The pins are of ¼-in diameter and are ¼ in high. They and their spacing precisely match holes punched in the sheets of drafting material. This system of registration bar and punch ties all the production elements together—architect, engineer, and reprographics plant. Standard registration bars are used on drafting boards, copyboards, film holders, and flatbed contact printers. To control larger sheets, nine- and eleven-pin bars are available. Also available are systems that use combinations of round and slotted holes to gain a certain amount of additional holding power and accuracy. Securing a bar to a drafting board is a simple matter of aligning the bar near the top edge of the board, with the pins toward the bottom, with the straightedge or drafting machine. The punched sheet of film is pressed snugly over the pins, which are usually made with top edges slightly beveled.

TECHNIQUE

Production efficiency can be analyzed by comparing floor plan development by the traditional and overlay-register methods.

Traditional Method   In the traditional method of drafting, production is geared to the recording of all pertinent data that can be safely fitted on a sheet. The final result obtained by this method may not be as hoped if an intuitive, unplanned approach is taken from beginning to end. The critical aspect of the traditional method is often the difficulty of achieving consistently good productivity. What is required is a high level of competency possessed by the

TABLE 7-1 Guide to Film and Paper

Material	Thick-ness, mils	Surface	Use	Eraser
			Drafting Film	
Film	4	Matte one side	Preferred for drafting	Vinyl
Film	4	Matte two sides	Occasional drafting use such as a plan on one side and a grid on the back. Not as translucent as matte one side	Vinyl
Film	4	No matte; smooth both sides	Has no draftable surface, useful for appliqués and press-on graphic arts materials	None
			Photosensitized Contact and Projection-Type Film	
Film	4	Matte one side	Preferred for further development by hand drafting: Wash-off type Fixed line	Vinyl Moistened vinyl two-part chemical
Film	4	Matte two sides	Photo image one side, draftable surface the other side	Same as above
Film	4	No matte	Used for composites	None
			Diazo-Sensitized Film and Vellum	
Film	3	Matte one side	Preferred for further development by hand drafting	Choice of eraser or chemical solution
Film	3	Matte two sides	Occasional use, sepia line	Same as one side
Film	3	No matte	Lowest cost for throwaways, base sheet copies, and composites	None
Film	2	Smooth	Adhesive-backed material for time-saving shortcuts such as scissors drafting	
		Matte	Same as above with draftable surface	Choice of eraser or chemical solution
Vellum	—	Matte two sides	For prints, or intermediates, for checking and review. Has draftable matte surface	Choice of eraser or chemical solution
Film	2	Smooth	Adhesive-backed material for time-saving scissors drafting	
		Matte one side	Same as above with draftable surface	Choice of moist eraser or chemical solution
Vellum	—	Matte two sides	For intermediate use for check and review printing. Draftable matte surfaces	Choice of chemical solution or medium eraser

These are general descriptions of available materials that are actually more complex than described here. For example, film for contact photoreproductions can be either a negative type or a direct positive type that saves one step. There are also times when it may be advisable to obtain a reverse-read reproduction, which results in a better whiteprint than a right-read reproducible. The best advice for an architect is to consult with the reprographic specialist and determine the best and most economical methods of using photosensitive products. Other considerations are the following:

1. Sensitized emulsions, whether silver or diazo, can be factory-applied on either the draftable matte side or on the smooth side of a film with a matte surface on the other side. The reproducible the architect receives can have the image line on either the matte surface or the smooth side. If the image line is photographically recorded on the smooth side and the architect plans to draw on the matte side, that fact must be made clear to the reprographic specialist to prevent a print that may be the reverse of what the architect wants.

2. When three sheets of material are to be composited, it is important to avoid having more than one thickness of film between ink-to-emulsion surfaces.

3. When a number of sheets are to be composited for a diazo reproducible, the most important sheet should be closest to the diazo-sensitized surface, because the sheets farthest from the sensitized surface will have fainter lines. The effect is similar to that of screening.

4. Coffee and other liquids and cigarettes must be kept away from film and vellum. Sheets must be clean if prints are to be clear.

talented—quality and speed that are often beyond the capacity of others in the same drafting room. Productivity then becomes too dependent upon one person or a few persons. When it does, quality is likely to lessen as the number of people involved with the development of a sheet increases. This is an unbalanced organization that often is made to work by having the most skillful people find the solutions to problems that are then handed on to the less skillful to put on drawings. A balanced project team relies on its skillful members for leadership, training, and use of an effective system such as overlay drafting.

Another undesirable result of the traditional method is a "presentation drawing" created to suit the drafter rather than the needs of the constructor. Also undesirable is the drawing that has only a small amount of detail, all gathered to the far-left side of the sheet and some of it almost lost under the binding margin. Persons in the field like to find details starting from the right side of the drawing.

Overlay-Register Method Drawings produced by the overlay-register method can be structured in any manner that suits every party concerned: the drafter, architect, owner (for fast-track methods), and builder (for more accurate job pricing and coordination of trades).

SHEET DESIGN

Sheet design for the overlay-register technique is modified as follows:

1. Project numbers should appear on all base sheets, overlays, and composites to provide identification at all times and keep sheets from getting lost and misfiled.

2. Borders should have small arrowheads spotted at center points of sides and top and bottom for photographic alignment if the sheets are to be microfilmed.

3. When offset half-size printing is being considered, a graphic scale should be used in addition to the normal scale. It should appear in two places: the final scale in the title block or under layouts and the scale of the original drawing, usually shown freehand outside the border. When the printed drawings have a full-size graphic scale, they are, of course, full-size and not half-size drawings.

4. Lettering style is still an individual choice, but lettering size is critical for half-size printing. The minimum lettering height for reduction of drawings for offset printing and also for microfilming is ⅛ in.

5. Revisions must be identified consistently in order to make certain that all engineers are working with the latest issue of base sheets.

Drawing titles and numbers have unusual importance in the overlay system. For one thing the system imposes special requirements for double numbering:

1. Drawing numbers, which are normally an office standard.

2. Register numbers, which will involve decisions as to how to create them and where to place them on sheets.

When a project is complete, all drawings will have been numbered in the normal office manner. Some of the drawings will have been produced by the conventional one-sheet method; others will be composites—combinations of base sheets and overlays. The individually prepared sheets need positive identification to assure that they will be correctly included in the composite.

Double Numbering   All the final composite drawings of a project receive two drawing numbers:

1. A typical drawing number according to the office standard such as A-1, S-4, or E-10.

2. A register number that is a code, a combination of numbers and letters. The code can become quite long whenever a composite is made up of four or more sheets, since it must identify every base sheet and overlay that is a part of the composite. It is the architect's option whether the register number appears in the final printing or is erased before printing. It should, however, be recorded somewhere to make certain that the arrangement of sheets can be repeated in the future.

Numbering and identifying base sheets and overlays involve the following decisions:

- Which overlay gets the drawing number that will appear on the composite?

- How should sheet identification code data, numbers and letters, be placed on sheets to avoid conflicts of data?

- How and where should other sheet design data, such as project number, initials of drafters, and revision data, be placed on base sheets and overlays?

To avoid confusion, simple rules and methods such as the following should be adopted:

1. Establish a master drawing index that lists as many drawings, by titles and drawing numbers, as possible.

2. Establish a list of base sheets and overlays by title and number. Confirm that there are no floor-to-floor positioning conflicts when multistory buildings are concerned.

3. Establish a standard location for the project number on all sheets.

4. Establish the design and location of the register number. Usually it is a rectangular block located along the bottom of the sheet or along the binding strip in a vertical position.

5. Establish ways to place revision dates and numbers on base sheets and overlays to assure that all overlays are worked in conjunction with the current, proper issue of base sheets.

6. Assign number or letter identifiers to base sheets and overlays in the order the sheets are prepared. Position the numbers on the sheets in the order the sheets are prepared. This is the first step in making certain there will be no conflicts when sheets are superimposed. At the same time, the sheets that create the composite are identified.

A complex arrangement of sheets will therefore have what appears to be a complicated numbering system. Consider, for example, an electric lighting plan prepared in conjunction with an architectural base sheet and overlays. Each sheet will accumulate a register number or code as shown in Figure 7-1. Lighting plan E-21 has the register number b, A-10, A-11, E-21, which signifies its production from floor plan base sheet b, room name and number overlay A-10, reflected ceiling plan overlay A-11, and electric lighting overlay E-21.

When all the sheets are superimposed for checking and coordination, the numbers will be aligned without conflict. It should be evident, however, that architectural overlays will not have their normal final drawing numbers and titles in proper position until the drawings are ready for final compositing. Otherwise that data may conflict with engineer's data. As Figure 7-1 shows, the overlays for room names and numbers and the ceiling plan also have final drawing numbers that are in proper position within the register number block but could be in conflict if either appeared in the box occupied by E-21.

An overlay-register numbering system should be viewed as little more than a problem-solving device that has a logical order. The system should be kept as simple as possible, and with some use it will become as familiar as the typical numbering system.

BASE SHEET

The base sheet, a primary element of the system, is usually prepared by hand on matte-surfaced film. It can also be prepared by computer, pasteup, or photoreproduction. It is the basis for the development of a series of drawings, so its content is limited to information for a floor plan: columns, partitions, doors, windows, and vertical transportation. With such information on it, the floor plan is referred to as a background or reference sheet.

The term "base sheet" can have different meanings. Typically it is taken to mean a layout, a floor plan. It may also mean a sheet that contains information common to several sheets. Using the electric lighting plan as an example, the identities of base sheet and overlay could be as follows:

1. The lighting plan. A sheet with information that applies only to light fixture layout. That makes it an *overlay*.

2. Ceiling plan. A sheet with information common to several sheets: architectural floor plan, ceiling register plan for HVAC, and the lighting plan. So it can be termed a *base sheet*.

3. Room names and numbers. Another sheet that has information common

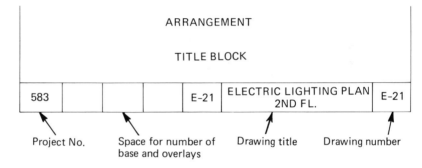

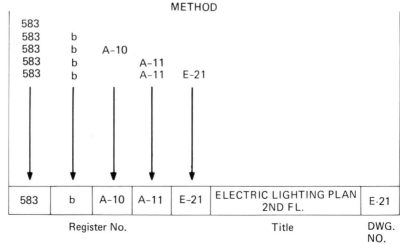

FIGURE 7-1 Register number system.

to several sheets: plumbing, HVAC, electric lighting, and architectural floor plan. So it also can be termed a *base sheet.*

If those definitions were taken to their logical limit, a floor plan base sheet composited with the room name sheet and the ceiling plan would produce a composite made up of *three base sheets. No overlays!* What that teaches us is that the important thing is not proper terminology; instead, it is the correct identification of sheets. Keep the understanding clear; keep the system simple.

Preparation   As described in Chapter 6, all polyester film for base sheets and overlays must be punched before drafting is started. Punching is critical to the success of the system. Punching is a service usually provided by the reprographics facility, and it will be necessary on drafting film, diazo-sensitized film, photosensitized film, film negatives, and offset printing plates, that is, on all sheets in the project set that will be produced by the overlay-register technique. Punching should result in full, clean holes that match perfectly the pins on the registration bars.

The registration of prepunched overlays and base sheets to an accuracy of approximately 0.003 in is possible under normal conditions. That is consistent with the stability of the material. Certain cautions must be observed: sheets must be punched in an organized way to avoid material damage and such errors as multiple or confusing registration holes. One cause for trouble could be punching some sheets with matte surface up and others with smooth sides up. When there is doubt, the questionable sheets should be set aside for use on projects or drawings with which registration is not involved.

Copy Production   Once diazo or photo copies start coming out, activity within a design project intensifies dramatically. Team members take advantage of the simpler production features of the overlay-register technique. Each engineer and consultant gets a head start on special design work, because much of the drafting has already been done on the base sheet, and design can start from there. The opportunity to get a project underway quickly and efficiently is a major advantage of the overlay system.

The engineer will, therefore, need a copy of the base sheet. A photographic copy offers the sharpest, clearest image lines, but its cost is much higher than that of a diazo copy. For a base sheet of background data on which an engineer will draft an overlay, quality is not nearly as vital as accuracy. Exceptional quality is saved for final printing. The base sheet normally has no further use once an overlay design is complete and ready for compositing for check printing and progress review. It is then filed until a revised copy is issued by the architect as a result of corrections of errors and design changes. The current issue is retained and filed separately from project drawings, and the void issues are discarded.

Both diazo and photo copies can be obtained with either a fixed hard line or an erasable image line. As a rule, however, a copy of a base sheet will not have to be changed; in fact, in most instances the architect should not permit changes on base sheets as a matter of policy and for absolute control of quality.

It thus makes little difference which product is to be used unless cost is the determinant.

When to make copies   The rules are simple. The first issues of base sheet copies serve to get engineering analysis and computations underway as soon as possible. These issues should be fully developed as complete layouts, but they should be unpretentious so far as dimensions, space names and numbers, and notes are concerned. That information might conflict with engineering layouts. At times it will be helpful to also distribute marked-up whiteprints together with polyester film diazo copies of the base sheet bearing quick freehand notes of useful information such as space titles and numbers or perhaps dimensions.

Follow-up copies of base sheets are needed whenever significant data changes have been made. The question of how often to issue copies of base sheets is related to the means of communicating changes to team members. That can range from telephone calls to paper copies of small area changes to full-size film copies. Economic factors must be evaluated against the chances of changes not being accurately recorded. The problem of communicating changes with the overlay system is little different than with traditional methods. Breakdowns in communications will occur no matter what method of communicating is used. That most projects suffer badly from weaknesses in communication, inept coordination, and failure to make changes after being informed of them is well known. Close attention to this problem of management can have an important impact on progress as well as on quality.

How many copies to make.   Careless printing of unneeded copies can become expensive. "Throwaways" should refer only to copies that have proved their use, not to copies that didn't have to be made in the first place. There will be occasions when a study of layout changes can be done over a whiteprint while another staff member is preparing an overlay for other features. That, of course, is normal procedure that applies to conventional production methods as well. The goal should be to economize as much as possible by first planning the project as thoroughly as possible.

OVERLAYS

An architect who was about to activate a project and searched for a way, tool, or method that would safeguard profit would be unlikely to find anything comparable with the overlay. Here is a remarkably versatile device for controlling quality, time, and cost. In construction there is a certain cost balance between labor and material; in architecture there is no such balance. Technical and professional labor costs far outweigh the costs of material and services. The latter have only a minor impact on profit and loss; any savings to be realized must be gained from technical-labor-dominated production. But the first need in a project is not for production; it is for solutions to architectural problems of planning, design, and detail. They must be contained first. The staff must become proficient architectural problem solvers before it tries to master production technology, which is so much easier to do.

Trying to pinpoint areas where savings can be made is the primary concern of production management, and nothing can match the help of the overlay in this connection. For example, when the overlay is the primary base for productivity, the question is whether the engineer gains before the architect does. The answer is no, not at all! It is the architect who gains first. After all, whenever some element of production is under control, no matter what that element may be, the architect benefits. Every single production element is the architect's concern.

Production of construction documents represents the critical part of the cost of a project. As complex as a project is, every single element is subject to examination of the basic problem and the management of time. Each drawing represents profit as well as cost. Too often profit is looked upon as an element that appears only at the end of the production process. The value of cost-saving measures diminishes with time; as a project nears its end, it becomes almost impossible to save money and salvage profit. The incomparable importance of the overlay is that it represents cost savings up front, where it is needed the most!

Up-front Cost Savings   Here is how up-front cost savings occur:

1. A copy of the base sheet, containing only essential layout data, goes to engineers so they can get an early start on design. Logical, orderly time-saving development procedures are thereby encouraged. This is an up-front savings in time.

2. When an engineer receives a copy of the base sheet, a large part of the drafting effort is out of the way before a single line is drawn on the overlay by the engineer. That is another up-front savings. Now multiply that savings by the number of floors of a project and the number of engineers, consultants, and other team members involved with the procedure and up-front savings accelerate.

3. Correcting drafting errors is negative work that needs control because it detracts from profit. Efficient correction technique reduces the impact on profit. When layout changes are made on separate base sheets and overlays, only the essential data gets erased, not all the nearby data that might be in the way. It is not necessary, for example, to go through the entire procedure of changes—layout, dimensions, space titles, material indications, equipment, and furniture. If six data elements are involved, every item that can be spared from the erasing procedure is a cost savings. These are not only up-front savings, they occur periodically during the progress of the project.

4. When the architect assumes the responsibility for correcting a floor plan base sheet, all the engineers are spared that task. Multiply the number of floor plans that are likely to be changed by the number of disciplines involved, put a dollar figure on each part, and count up the cost savings.

5. One floor of a project will have many layouts for architectural and engineering purposes. The architect knows only one plan has to be checked for accuracy. All the others are copies, and so they are automatically checked. Here up-front savings come from simpler coordination.

6. Up-front savings come from using one base sheet for other professional services on the same project. Examples are an overlay showing presentation data for business development purposes and an overlay illustrating fire exits, fire walls, zones, and so on. The latter answers an often overlooked need for coordination of architect and government agency.

7. Up-front cost savings occur every time someone discovers a job shortcut.

Creativity may be the dominant interest in a practice, but productivity cannot be overlooked if creative efforts are to be ensured of rewards. It is productivity that has the power to safeguard profit. And the key to productivity is the overlay, the versatile, productive overlay! Just like the interest on a discount loan, management should take profit right off the top and then defy any member of the team to threaten profitability. But to stand up to a challenge, the team should have the means of coping with threats to profitability.

COMPOSITES

The artistic, innovative architect sends a drawing to the printer. It is a complete drawing made up of a base sheet and overlays. The printer delivers one print to the client and another to the engineer.

The same drawing, the same day, but each receives a drawing that looks entirely different from the other! The client marvels at a clear, clean, skillfully prepared drawing that looks like a work of art. The engineer also admires the drawing he receives, even though it is defaced with scribbled notes, marks, and symbols. To the engineer also it is a work of art—but of a different kind. The engineer views it as an innovative means of communicating instructions in a time-saving, orderly, concise manner!

How and why would an architect appear to damage an important, valuable drawing, the one sent to the engineer?

Or was it damaged?

Of course not; it was all done by the magic of the overlay, the versatile overlay. And it is a simple matter for the architect to retrieve the overlay marked up in pencil with notes, clean it up, and use it all over again.

The lesson to be learned is that with the overlay system a composite can be whatever the architect, client, engineer, builder or government agency needs it to be for an individual purpose.

FORMAT SHEETS

A format is a precut sheet of drafting material that has been printed with border, title block, and other basic project data (Figure 7-2). It is designed just as carefully as any other feature of an architectural project, because a well-designed format sheet represents a definite cost savings. Its advantage lies in the savings in technical labor time through the elimination of stamping or hand drafting title blocks and borders and various items of general information.

The format sheet is produced in either of two ways: by photography or by

FIGURE 7-2 Format sheet. Formats for typical office use are press runs on either vellum or polyester film. The purchaser has the option of smooth base or a matte surface on one or both sides. (Jewell, Downing & Associates)

offset printing. Offset printing is fast and is far less expensive than photography, which can only produce one sheet at a time.

Design   The format sheet master—the art needed by the printer—is prepared in ink, preferably on polyester film. Hand drafting, pasteup, scissors, or photodrafting can be used. An alternative to the architect taking the time to prepare the art for the sheet is to have a commercial printer prepare the sheet mock-up under the architect's direction.

The size is usually a multiple of the 8½- by-11 in module, which will be a standard detail sheet filing size. The maximum recommended sheet size is 30 by 42 in, which is an off-module size. Marks around the perimeter of the sheet identify the 8½- by 11-in modules, and arrow points at the centers of sides, top, and bottom serve as camera targets if the sheets are to be microfilmed.

Subdivisions of 8½- by 11-in also are established to facilitate sheet organization of details, schedules, title block, legends, general notes, and symbols. Title blocks are designed to meet special requirements; those of the architect will differ from those of government agencies. The designs may be either an office standard or a special for a particular project. The latter may contain more exact data such as the project name, location, key plans, compass points, approval needs, drawing numbers, and register number blocks. Lettering methods will vary from freehand to typing done on special typewriters.

After the sheet is designed, it is photographed either by contact or process camera unit to obtain a full-size negative or reduction negative. From the negative an offset printing plate is made. A volume run is made on paper, vellum, or the polyester film that is mandatory for overlay system use. The cost of commercial printing is usually based on a minimal run of 100 sheets.

When the overlay system is to be used, fewer copies of the format sheet are needed. One format sheet punched for registration is usually all that is necessary for compositing with any series of base and overlay sheets.

The full-size negatives may be filed for subsequent reuse. The design can be changed for use in future projects by masking, opaquing, and splicing in of new data. A certain number of sheets will also be drafted by hand. The number of format sheets needed on a project can be established with some accuracy by noting on the master drawing list, with the initial F, which drawings are to be drafted on format sheets.

CHAPTER EIGHT

Application to Design

This chapter covers production techniques that augment professional services at the onset of project development. Also covered are some other services rendered later in the project, depending on its type and size. The subjects include schematics and their development and special applications of the overlay system.

SCHEMATICS

Schematic drawings are the first-stage graphics that activate a project. They are prepared to illustrate to the client the proposed solution to a building problem by the use of one or more drawings and sketches. They may cover site design as well as building projects and be in either of two forms, diagrammatical or formal.

Diagrammatical style   Simple single-line drawings are often the choice of architects. Some are done freehand, which, if acceptable to the client, should provide some cost savings for both client and architect. The freehand single-line drawings evolve from the usual freehand sketching exercises.

Formal schematics   Freehand schematics may not look as professional as the client might expect. Then it is advisable to produce formal drawings in either single or double line. Double-line schematics prepared in a formal manner can be the basis for the ideal production system: one drawing that continues in use from schematics all the way through design development to working drawing phases.

Development Schematic design methodology is probably the least technically developed architectural service. Quality performance applies to both artistic design and solutions to client's building problems, and the two goals are not necessarily approached from the same direction. The aesthetic aspect of project appearance is typically centered around an all-drawing effort. Often the same tactic is used for a solution to a building problem, the goal being one drawing or a series of drawings (schematics), to be discarded at a later time after being used for preparation of design development drawings.

Another and usually much more efficient approach to design schematics is a logical analytical process. Although there is no universal understanding of what constitutes a perfect design and problem-solving procedure, the following outline covers many project-planning essentials:

1. Establish a checklist of data and services provided by the client: program, consultants, and up-to-date survey of the legal, physical, and utility aspects of the site.

2. Confirm what the client expects to receive in drawings and such other presentation materials as models and renderings.

3. Confirm input from others. Know their authorities and responsibilities, clients and staff assistants, consultants, engineers, programmers, and specialists.

4. Verify that design limitations are clearly defined: budget, program, time schedule, zoning, ordinances, economics, social, and community.

5. Confirm the accuracy of the program and all required approvals: client, architect-in-charge, consultants, and engineers.

6. Compare the floor area of the program and the budget for feasibility. Also include site work, associated work, and services.

7. Check the feasibility of the siting. Consider orientation, views, main and secondary entrances, drives, parking, loading, exterior electrical and mechanical requirements, fire department, public transportation, and future expansion.

8. Study building height requirements according to floor area, site restrictions, zoning, future vertical expansion, and story heights.

9. Block out such economical considerations as building height and size, configuration of bays, structural and mechanical systems, and materials.

10. Establish a plan outline. Consider limitations of programmed floor area, interior functions, bay configurations, structure and mechanics, and codes, ordinances, and community restrictions.

11. Confirm preliminary requirements for auxiliary spaces: lobbies, circulation, vertical transportation, toilet rooms, mechanical equipment, and egress.

12. Analyze statement of space needs; establish simple functional space diagrams; consider use of planning methods such as bubble diagrams; plan control charting.

13. Evaluate spatial and sizing relations by the use of some such technique as value engineering.

14. Modify space plans for sizing, proportion, and fit to bays, units, and multiples.

15. Review planning goals for interior and exterior: services, function, cost, and artistic freedom for exterior design.

16. Determine drawing production methods such as overlay technique.

17. Consider special production techniques: pasteup, appliqués, overlay, and material indications.

18. Review the need for special illustrations: interior walls, floors, ceiling, special equipment, and furnishings.

19. Translate findings to schematic drawings. Avoid being too technical for the client, but make certain no vital factors are hidden from the client or not easy for the client to understand.

Photoreproduction   Schematics are subject to change both during development and after client acceptance. Typically they are prepared at small scale to save time, facilitate change, and help keep design expense within budget. Formal drawings look more professional than freehand drawings, but the extra development time that they require when done at small scale could increase the cost of working drawings if the formal-style schematics must be done again at larger scale in the working drawing phase.

That practice, of drawing at small scale, say $^1/_{16}$ in, and then redoing everything at a larger scale, say $\frac{1}{8}$ in, at a later phase, has been questioned. Redrawing, obviously, detracts from profitability, and if done by hand, it introduces almost endless possibilities for error. If small-scale formal schematics are decided on, the change from one scale to another can be made by photography. The translation of graphic data from one scale to another, say, from $^1/_{16}$ to $\frac{1}{8}$ in, can be free of error and can be done in less time and at less cost without any hand-drafting effort.

Another way to think of redrawing is as scale changing, a routine bit of modern photographic technology using the reprographic process camera-projector unit. By combining the features of the overlay system and photographic scale-changing methodology, basic documentation for schematic, design development, and working drawings can be produced with outstanding clarity, quality, and at lower cost than by resorting to hand drafting.

The production technique illustrated by Figures 8-1 to 8-3 combines photography and hand drawing. It is used to produce a small-scale schematic drawing and also a photographically enlarged version for use as a design development drawing to be continued through to the working drawing phase. Although it is primarily concerned with floor plans, the technique is also applicable to such other project elements as exterior elevations. The somewhat elaborate example illustrated here shows how a large project might be developed by using two sheets to contain the entire floor plan at $\frac{1}{8}$-in scale.

Drawing phase   Development during the drawing phase is as follows:

1. Draw at the proper scale for the design development phase. The schematic drawing at $^1/_{16}$-in scale will evolve as a photographic product. It will be a

small-scale copy of the hand-drawn original on film with a moist-erasable line image.

2. The plan is developed by following a design methodology approach. Because of its large size, it is divided into two parts on separate sheets.

3. A full-size format sheet punched for registration may be used, and then a framing grid or plan template is drawn at working drawing scale.

4. Either draw by hand or obtain a photographic copy of the template made on film with a moist-erasable line image.

5. On one of the grid-template sheets, draw half of the floor plan at ⅛-in scale. This might be the right half of the plan (Figure 8-1).

6. After the plan is drawn, place the sheet on a few pins of the registration bar. On the remaining pins the second sheet can be positioned over the first one. The positioning will be a temporary one for determining alignment points.

7. Place the second, prepunched sheet of drafting film part way over the first sheet and snap the punched holes over the pins on the bar. The top sheet should lap the bottom sheet a few, but not too many, inches. Make certain the plan can be centered on the sheet. Establish and mark alignment points and match liner on the top sheet. The same marks will previously have been established on the bottom sheet, the right half of the plan (Figure 8-1).

8. Remove both sheets; reinstall the second sheet on the pin bar and proceed with drawing the left half of the floor plan (Figure 8-2). Omit notes, dimensions, space names; these go on overlays.

9. The two sheets can serve as base sheets for the design development drawings after acceptance of the schematics by the client.

Photoreproduction phase Next comes the production of a single sheet with both halves of the plan (Figures 8-1 and 8-2) perfectly combined into a single ¹/₁₆-in plan suitable for presentation to a client (Figure 8-3). Appropriate data are added on either the base sheet or overlays.

Production of the complete drawing is by photographic technology. The equipment used has scale-changing capability; an example is the overlay process camera-projector unit shown in Figure 6-5, together with pin registration techniques. In clarity and accuracy, the product will match a professionally prepared drawing. The original sheets are assumed to be of 30- by 42-in size, and they are photographed in the same order as they were drawn:

1. The first sheet drawn (Figure 8-1) is fitted to the pins of one registration bar mounted on a vertical copyboard. The sheet is photographed, and the image is recorded on a reduction negative punched for registration.

2. The negative is then approved for quality.

3. The second sheet drawn (Figure 8-2) is fitted to the registration pins over the first sheet placed and photographed on the copyboard. The second sheet, the left half of the floor plan, is so placed that it overlaps the sheet underneath and all previously noted alignment and match lines are coordinated as they

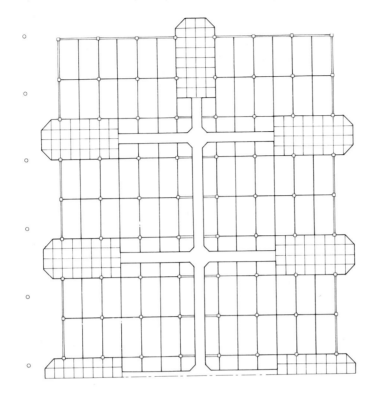

FIGURE 8-1 Right half of a two-part plan.

1. Draw grid, columns, and perimeter walls of right half of plan.

2. Photograph on pin bar mounted on copyboard. Obtain reduction negative.

3. Project negative back to sheet film on pin bar. Use as grid template for left-hand part of plan, or consider reverse copy for use as left-hand part.

4. To get match line orientation when hand drafting plan sheets, consider use of nine- or eleven-pin registration bar.

5. Draw only basic layout data; place other data on overlays.

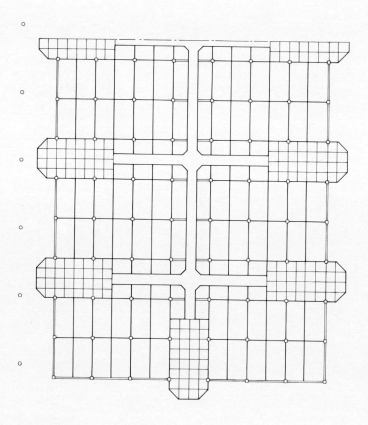

FIGURE 8-2 Left half of a two-part plan.

1. Either draw the plan or use a reverse film photo-copy of the right half. Registration and match lines must coincide.

2. Draw only basic layout data. Place other data on overlays.

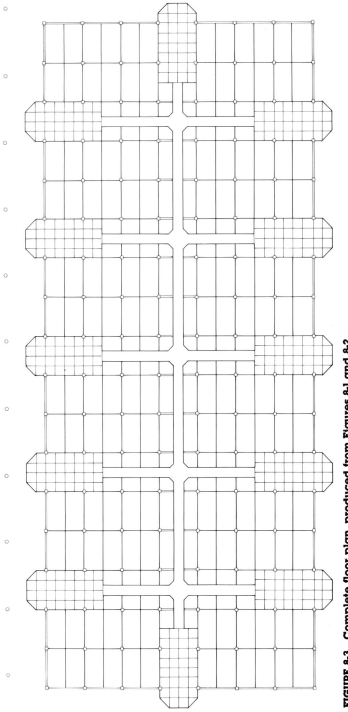

FIGURE 8-3 Complete floor plan, produced from Figures 8-1 and 8-2.

1. Camera-projector unit is positioned for scale changing to record image at $^1/_{16}$-in scale. An eleven-pin bar helps provide alignment.

2. A full-size sheet of photosensitive film is mounted on copyboard.

3. Right half of plan, Figure 8-1, is projected onto sheet.

4. Left half of plan, Figure 8-2, is projected onto sheet.

5. The sheet, after processing, becomes a mechanically produced drawing, a floor plan at $^1/_{16}$-in scale. Related data is prepared by hand on overlays.

were originally. It may be necessary to readjust the second registration bar to get perfect match of alignment points and match lines. An eleven-pin bar would work well with this technique.

4. The first sheet (Figure 8-1, right half of the floor plan) is removed from the copyboard and put aside.

5. A new reduction negative, prepunched, is placed on the pins of the film holder.

6. The second sheet (Figure 8-2) is photographed. The negative is removed, processed, and checked for quality. If it is not acceptable, another negative is put back into the camera and a new shot is made. The second sheet is removed from the copyboard.

7. After photography is complete, the projection copy-making technique is used. The process unit is changed from the photographic function to the projection function and moved into the precise position for projecting images to a scale smaller than the original. In this case it is from ⅛ in down to 1/16 in.

8. Previously two original drawings had been photographed separately on the copyboard; now a single sheet of photosensitized polyester film is pinned to the registration bar on the copyboard. At the architect's option, this sheet may have a smooth or a draftable matte surface.

9. The negatives of the two previously photographed originals (Figures 8-1 and 8-2) are, one at a time, placed back into the film holder of the unit. In turn they are projected back onto the single sheet of photosensitive film mounted on the copyboard. When both images have been recorded, the two plans will emerge in perfect alignment as a single plan at 1/16-in scale.

10. When both negatives have been projected, the film is removed from the registration bar on the copyboard and processed to bring out the image. At the architect's option the image can be moist or fixed line.

11. The photographer files the negatives. To the architect go the two original sheets and the new single-sheet "original." The image on the latter is a complete drawing, properly positioned and to accurate scale, with dense black lines of outstanding quality. It is ready for any final touches for presentation to the client as a schematic drawing.

Cost Benefits   The combination technique described above has these advantages over drawing exclusively by hand:

- Reduction in handwork
- Relief from scale-changing errors and omissions
- Less need for coordination
- Lower cost

The cost-benefit analysis is as follows:

The photographically created drawing will cost approximately $75. That is the cost of two negatives, a single sheet of photosensitive film and services. It will vary, and the architect should obtain up to date service prices. This product becomes an original suitable for whiteprinting for checking, review, and submittal to the client.

Now, the cost figures can be related to the cost of hand drafting the same amount of information. The comparison provides a guide to a decision to use photoreproduction. As a rule of thumb, it is feasible to use photoreproduction when it might take as long as 2½ hrs to produce the same work by hand.

Another factor is the amount of data shown on the final drawing. If it is more than that shown in Figure 8-3, the cost of drawing by hand might be increased but the cost of photo services would be unchanged. The amount of data to be recorded on the sheet has no effect on the cost of services unless some materials must be blocked out when the sheet is photographed or the negatives require considerable retouching. Then cost figures may have to be adjusted.

The cost figures are related to the architect's needs. If engineers and consultants are involved in preparation of schematics and each would ordinarily be required to prepare all floor plans by hand, technical labor costs will increase considerably. On the other hand, photoreproduction costs would actually decrease. If the photographic cost of the single-sheet schematic plan at $^1/_{16}$-in scale is $75, additional copies of that same plan can be obtained at less cost in either of two ways, each of which could produce an erasable image line.

1. By photography. Additional copies on polyester wash-off film might cost $30 each.

2. By diazo. Film copies produced on a flatbed printer would cost about $10.

OVERLAY SYSTEM APPLICATIONS

Advanced production technology is applicable to more than the production of small-scale schematics. The same photographically produced drawing can serve other early design purposes as well as meet a number of needs that arise later in project development. Examples of the latter are presentations, project phasing, demolition work, and interior graphics.

Schematics   The following are some of the advantages of producing a set of schematics by using overlay-register techniques.

1. One drawing in the set may simply be the floor plan base sheet layout without any associated data such as space identification.

2. Another drawing may be a composite of the base sheet together with a notation overlay. If the keynote method is used, explanatory notes can be more definitive and clearer than notes placed directly on the plan.

3. Another drawing may be a composite of the base sheet together with an overlay identifying special-use areas, fire zones, departments, etc.

4. Other drawings, composites of the floor plan base sheet and engineering concept overlays, would complete the set.

These drawings provide clear, easy-to-understand design features that extend from engineering to more elaborate presentation methods.

Presentations Artistic presentations present another opportunity for the application of overlay-register techniques and the small-scale schematic development plan illustrated by Figures 8-1 to 8-3. Efficient preparation and low cost are the benefits to be gained.

The punched base sheet is secured to the pins of a registration bar on the drafting board and with it special overlays are prepared on polyester drafting film. The overlays are in addition to those that meet the special demands of clients, consultants, zoning agencies, building departments, and fire departments. Graphics can be added by use of press-on materials: tapes, letters, shading, and material textures. The base sheet and special overlays can be composited for a variety of presentations.

Another valuable presentation device made available by the overlay-register technique is the transparency for overhead projection. Any drawing that has been photographically recorded on a small-size reduction negative can also be reproduced on 8½- by 11-in pin-registered positive transparencies. Production is directly from the small negative, usually on acetate film and punched for registration.

All base sheets and overlays produced on transparencies have the same precise registration and alignment as the original hand-drawn tracings. They can be produced in a broad range of colors to help make conference presentations easier and more interesting. They provide the opportunity for more people to become involved and to get greater input from each. The manner of projection offers opportunities that are not available by any other means. The transparency can be screened in any manner that may be useful: base to overlay such as floor plan, structural to mechanical, and so on. Three-pin registration bars are available for this purpose.

Project Phasing When project phasing is needed for planning and scheduling purposes, some problems are bound to come to mind:

- How to show phasing data clearly on drawings
- How to make phasing elements mesh together smoothly
- How to keep phasing during construction from becoming a financial nightmare

Some phasing elements that can create serious conflicts include:

- Demolition of unoccupied and unused areas
- Demolition of spaces that must remain in use for a certain time
- New construction in both occupied and unoccupied spaces
- Alterations of unoccupied, unused spaces
- Alterations of spaces to remain in operation

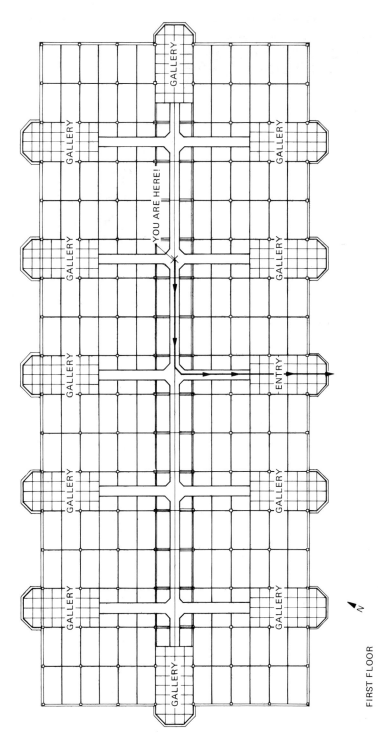

FIRST FLOOR

N

FIGURE 8-4 Buildings graphics for static display. This sheet is a photocopy of Figure 8-3. It does not have to be to scale. If used after construction is complete, it may require updating by hand. Formal lettering and other graphics can be placed on the copy or on overlays. The drawing is then ready as camera art for production of plastic-imbedded sheets to be framed or mounted for display purposes.

- Temporary relocation of spaces and areas to remain in operation while demolition, remodeling, or new construction takes place
- Materials and equipment to remain in place, to be removed for temporary storage and future reuse, or for salvage
- Temporary weatherproofing enclosures for vertical as well as horizontal expansion
- Vertical transportation: stairs, elevators, conveyor removal, replacement, and temporary operation

The first priority of phasing is to identify all elements. Then the overlay-register technique can be applied, usually after freehand sketching, to develop a workable plan for the benefit of the client and the constructor.

Demolition Work   The simplest way to explain demolition work is by a series of overlays. Appliqué material is used to identify, on overlays, existing conditions, removal work, and the sequence of work, all in such a way that the contractor can furnish the client with an economical cost of work.

Building Graphics   In some projects use may be found for graphics that show interior traffic and related information after construction work is complete. The overlay system has the capability of providing such graphics with a minimum of drafting production, as illustrated by Figure 8-4.

First the original schematic drawing (Figure 8-3) is updated to reflect as-built conditions. Then a series of overlays are prepared to record associated data and render such elements as walls, flooring, and space identification, street names, exits, vertical transportation, directories, and direction arrows.

The base sheet and the various overlays are then composited photographically and reproduced at the selected size. The product would be regarded as camera-ready art by companies specializing in screen processes. One technique is to print the drawing on specially absorbent paper which is then sandwiched in plastic sheets. The result is a strong rigid panel suitable for framing and installation at strategic points within a building such as elevator lobbies and corridor intersections. Products with colors integrated within the graphic panels also are available.

CHAPTER NINE

Application to Land Development

This chapter explains in detail how the overlay system is used to prepare drawings for the land development aspect of a construction project. This use ought to be particularly appealing to engineers because of its unlimited problem-solving potential. The system can be applied to the wide variety of design features involved with site work: topo survey, soil boring, erosion control, site utilities, site structures, grading, paving, landscaping, planting, plant layout, recreation facilities, and furniture. Few other areas of design offer the opportunity for so many uses of overlays with a variety of base sheets. Production work can be simplified and quality control facilitated.

Land development drawings range from a small project site plan to extremely complex plans for major projects. As the land work becomes more complicated, the job of deciding what information to show on the drawings and how to show it becomes more difficult. Indeed, site work drawings are potentially the most difficult drawings of the entire project. That is why the overlay system can be so effective. Work can be separated on numerous overlays and then be combined with base sheets to suit the requirements of the client, builder, architect, engineer, and code compliance people. The drawings can be simple graphic illustrations of land work or as complicated as necessary to reveal the extent of work.

This chapter is directed at the engineer, so there will be repetitions of text presented in other chapters. The fundamentals of the overlay system are described in Chapters 6 and 7.

BASE SHEETS

For the land design group of drawings, a layout plan serves as the base sheet. Related information is developed on overlays. From a production standpoint, it is important, when drafting a particular area of design, to avoid redrawing on an overlay any information already on the base sheet. With the overlay system, there is normally no need to repeat, on any overlay, a system, detail, or layout that is drawn on either the base sheet or any other overlay. Anything drawn on an overlay will, while the overlay is pin-registered with the base sheet, be perfectly aligned with all data on the base sheet.

The typical overlay containing a single design element will, of course, be incomprehensible to all but the person who prepared the overlay until the overlay is matched, through the reproduction process, with related data on the base sheet. Matching the base sheet and overlay produces the final objective, an efficiently prepared drawing of superior quality that is in all respects like one prepared in the conventional way. Before starting to use the overlay system for land development work, the reader should review Chapter 6.

Materials and Tools Drafting personnel will need the same drafting board and equipment that is needed for drawing in the conventional way. In addition, two components of the overlay system will be required: drafting film and registration bars, one for each drafter. All drawing will be done on sheets of polyester film with a draftable matte surface that have been punched beforehand with at least seven holes to fit pins of the registration bar. Refer to Table 7-1 for sheet film data.

The drafting film may be either full, project-size sheets or preprinted format sheets, depending on management plans for production of project drawings. If preprinted format sheets are used, care is needed. Format sheets that are not all punched at the same time may result in distortion of lines and letters on a composite produced for check printing, progress review, or final printing. When conflicts such as double line printing occur, the remedy is to use fewer format sheets and more blank sheets during drafting procedures or to opaque out conflicting lines on negatives. The latter is an expensive procedure.

Production Technique The base sheet is prepared on prepunched polyester film with a draftable matte surface on one side. But unless it is drawn in conjunction with, say, a format sheet, the registration bar does not have to be used. All information should be accurately placed on the base sheet within the limits of border, title block, and schedules that might appear on the final composited drawing. The techniques employed by the drafter to prepare a base sheet are a combination of formal line work and lettering—hand, press-on, or typewritten—and a considerable amount of freehand sketching.

A production goal is to prove out data before formalizing it on a drawing. All drawing activities are dependent on information derived from other team members, and the production drafter evaluates each drawing and detail and has that information at hand. Production efficiency is directly related to the drafter's ability to identify the data needed and communicate effectively with those who have the responsibility to provide it.

Development of the Layout Plan   First define the layout plan carefully and then decide what information is to be shown and how the sheet is to be prepared. Some of the features that might be shown include property lines and monuments, benchmarks, building outlines, streets, walks, drives, parking, zoning restrictions, limits of work, existing features to remain, and existing features to be removed. The base sheet layout plan is usually the most difficult sheet of the entire set of project drawings to define, and some care is needed in its preparation to avoid having to erase information and draw it back on an overlay sheet. The two primary problems involved are how to create the plan and how to place building information on it.

1. If an original tracing is available but cannot be reused:
   a. Make a completely new drawing by hand by tracing over the original on a punched full-size sheet of polyester drafting film with a matte surface. Relate the cost of hand work to the cost of a photore-production of the original data reworked by reprographics to delete unneeded data, blemishes, and so on.
   b. If the original survey cannot be adapted to the new project, have a new punched, full-size reproducible copy made with all unneeded information masked out. The copy should be made on clear base film if no further drafting work is needed; but if further drafting is required, it should be a reproducible with a moist-erasable image on a matte draftable surface.

2. When only a print of the survey is available:
   a. If the print is in good condition, have it copied on either clear base or matte surface film, as required.
   b. If the print is not in good condition, have it reproduced on film through restoration. This will require some masking, negative opaquing, and photographic artistry to beef up weak lines and images. When necessary, change the scale. Have the sheets punched.

Placing Buildings   Ground floor plans are often used on site layouts to facilitate organization, planning, and coordination of walks, parking, drives, utilities, and other exterior project features. A complete floor plan adds dimension to an overall view of the project; but the plan must be kept up to date, and that adds to the coordination responsibilities of architect and engineer. One solution is to use just perimeter profiling until the floor plan is complete and approved and then add it to the site layout plan. The ground floor plan can be placed on the site layout base sheet either by hand tracing or by photographing it and then pasting a print on the layout plan. It is possible to save time by photography, but the production costs of the options must be evaluated.

OVERLAY PREPARATION

Material and Tools Like base sheet development, overlay sheets are prepared on prepunched polyester film with a draftable matte surface on one side. Each drafting board will also require the standard seven-pin registration bar.

Production Technique The primary need in starting overlay production is reference data. Usually it is supplied by a base sheet layout plan, such as a topo survey, as background or underlayment. Either the hand-drawn original base sheet layout plan itself is used for overlay production or, if a number of persons are working on overlays, clear base copies can be made by diazo process. A small project staff may prefer to use just the original base sheet.

Production is begun by securing the punched base sheet layout plan, or a copy of it, to the pins of the standard registration bar. It is not necessary to attach the bar to the drafting board. The sheet is taped both to the bar, to keep sheets from slipping off, and the drafting board. Next a full-size punched sheet of matte surface drafting film is pressed down over the register pins on top of the base sheet. This sheet should have matte surface on just one side because it will be more transparent than a sheet with the matte on both sides. Drawing the overlay is like drawing the base sheet; it combines formal line and lettering work—hand, press-on, or typewritten—with freehand sketching.

It may be difficult to make progress and at the same time refrain from drawing information that has not been approved, but the proving-out technique should be a guiding principle. Some general guidelines for drafting overlay sheets are given in the following paragraphs, which primarily provide outlines of various overlay drawings and suggested information and data content. Before starting work, it is advisable to evaluate carefully the scope of any one overlay to determine the procedures best suited to the complete drawing or drawings. The possibility of simplifying drawing development to get fewer final drawings should not be overlooked.

Design Categories

Existing topo survey A reason for having the topo survey as an overlay produced either by hand tracing or as a reproducible is to retain as long as possible the opportunity to simplify the final compositing procedures. A topo survey with considerable contour data can easily become a very busy drawing.

Soil-boring data Soil-boring data is normally the client's legal responsibility. When it is prepared as a part of the contract for use by the engineers, it can be added to an overlay to guide the builder. The overlay can be made either by redrawing or by the cut-and-paste technique. It can then be composited with other project data, including structural foundation data, to convey the impact of soil conditions on foundation design and site work.

Soil erosion   A complete soil erosion drawing is developed in three sheets: the layout plan base sheet, a grading plan overlay, and an overlay prepared separately to show erosion control measures designed by the architect or the engineer with or without input from local authorities. The overlay will show erosion control objectives and methods of achieving them on the construction site during project activity and after construction is complete and the site is occupied.

Site utilities   A complete utilities drawing is developed in three sheets: the layout plan base sheet (Figure 9-1) as the background reference, a paving plan for drainage, and an overlay showing both above- and below-ground utility lines such as gas, water, sanitary sewer, steam, telephone, communications,

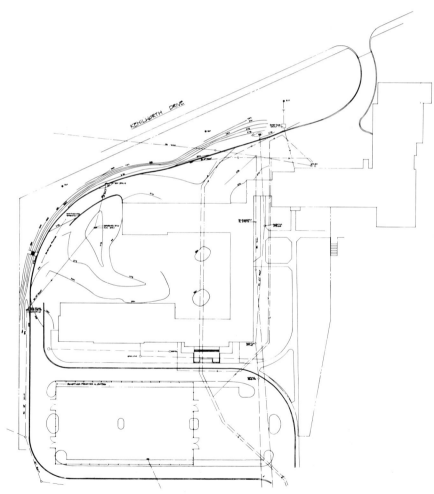

FIGURE 9-1   Site plan. The survey can be photographically produced as an overlay for further development and then combined photographically with the format sheet and possibly other data overlays. (Jewell, Downing & Associates, Architects)

and electric, and perhaps wells, test pits, and percolation tests. Although it is preferable to have all utilities on one sheet, complex site conditions may require separation on more than one overlay sheet. Schedules of structures and other features must be placed on overlay sheets so they do not conflict with data on other sheets.

Site structures A site structure drawing has special coordination purposes on major projects. It is prepared as an overlay in conjunction with structural layouts, site layout plan base sheet, and the grading and landscaping plan overlays. It coordinates the activities of earth moving, cut and fill, and scheduling and placing of concrete for various site features such as foundations for buildings, retaining walls, below-ground structures and manholes for electrical and other utilities, fence foundations, bases for flagpoles and light poles, storm drains, tunnels, and conduit systems. It thereby serves the architect well, particularly during the construction phase of services.

Grading plan The grading plan drawing is usually worked in conjunction with paving plan overlay and the layout plan base sheet. Other overlays may also be needed, and the grading plan overlay may require further development after the landscaping plan is completed.

Paving plan The paving plan overlay must be coordinated with other development overlays such as landscaping, utilities, and grading. Dimensions, details, and schedules, when they are needed, must be so located as not to conflict with associated data when the overlay is composited with the base sheet and other overlays to create the final drawing.

Landscape plan The landscape plan is composed of the layout plan base sheet, the paving overlay, and an overlay that shows planting, seeding, sodding, and schedules of plants. It might also include such features as outdoor furniture, bike paths, walks, cultivated areas, pools, trash containers, and signage.

Plant layout The plant layout is another drawing prepared for coordination purposes. It serves to control construction activities at various phases of the project. In conjunction with the layout plan base sheet, it locates contractor office trailers, material storage, property access, and off-limit areas. Interior as well as exterior spaces are shown. Appliqué materials and press-on tapes can make this a simple overlay to prepare.

Recreation facilities The recreation facilities drawing is prepared in conjunction with the layout plan base sheet and the landscaping and paving plans to show the locations of game layouts, playground plans and equipment, spectator seating, paths, and bike racks.

Phasing and demolition drawings The phasing and demolition drawings are used to expedite construction for fast-track projects. Press-on tapes and other appliqué materials are excellent ways to make features of the drawing easier to prepare and understand.

Composites

Which base sheets and overlays are to be combined as composites in the manner described in Chapter 6 is determined by the complexity of the project.

A simple way to arrive at decisions is to make sample, low-cost prints on the diazo whiteprinter. The ability to control quality and coordination by test runs is one of the most attractive features of the overlay system. It is, of course, available at any stage of the project.

Scissors drafting, appliqués, cut and paste, and photography can be usefully employed to enhance the quality of the final drawing. Photographs of existing site conditions and of models and renderings all help to make the professional drawings seem more interesting and easier to understand.

CHAPTER TEN

Architectural Drawings

The extensive advantages of the overlay system begin with production of the architectural drawings for a project. For the purposes of this book, the architectural work is divided into architectural drawings, alterations and additions, and details and special areas. It begins with the primary design elements of all the work: floor plans and associated overlays.

The production of a complete set of construction drawings has been called one of the most costly and time-consuming of any of the various development phases of a project. Some architects have an unrealistic impression of how expensive drawing production can be. To make matters worse, they often have only a vague idea of just how little money there is for the preparation of working drawings.

The Profit Picture   Suppose, for example, that an architect gets a commission of $50,000 for professional services in the design of a project. Obviously, not all of that fee goes into working drawings. The realistic breakdown of that $50,000 design commission goes like this:

Schematics	15%	$ 7,500
Design development	20%	10,000
Working drawings	40%	20,000
Bids	5%	2,500
Construction administration	20%	10,000
	100%	$50,000

The breakdown of the $20,000 for working drawings is as follows:

Architectural	18%	$ 9,000
Structural	6%	3,000
Mechanical and electrical	12%	6,000
Specifications	4%	2,000
	40%	$20,000

The 18 percent, or $9,000, is further broken down as follows:

Direct salaries and wages	6%	$3,000
Overhead	6%	3,000
Profit	6%	3,000
	18%	$9,000

That first $3,000 is the entire amount in the budget for the labor part of the architectural working drawing phase. The unreasonably low budget figure requires that a continuous close look be kept on production effort from schematics all the way through to bidding. The two goals are saving time for design and protecting profit. That the profit is far from automatic can be seen in Figure 10-1, which shows half a dozen wasteful ways in which the profit pie can be eaten into.

Obviously, the two initial production phases, schematics and design development, have to be kept within budget. Production shortcuts should be evaluated and decided upon during the project-planning phase that follows immediately upon activation of the project. If some schematic and design development production steps can be combined with the working drawing phase, pressure on profit can be shifted. Instead of its being entirely on the working drawing phase, the pressure can be applied at an earlier point of

FIGURE 10-1 The profit picture.

design development. That will improve the chances for a profitable project, no matter what the project size may be.

The architectural floor plan is the key drawing in the total development effort, and the manner in which it is produced—not just the initial effort, but all through its development—affects the progress made by other team members. Inefficient floor plan development is likely to hamper progress all the way through the project.

It is, of course, necessary that the production of all plans be pursued efficiently. Use should be made of the latest methods and management tools that produce results. Production planning and execution of this part of work should be stressed right from the beginning. Avoid a lazy start and a panic finish; concentrate on getting systems involved early.

DEFINITIONS

Design Development Before the production of working drawings for a project can get underway, the professional effort will have first proceeded through what is called the design development phase, which was discussed briefly in Chapter 5. The term seems to be difficult for some to understand. Just what does it mean?

It has been said to mean "to fix and describe the size and character of the project." That definition, by the American Institute of Architects (AIA), mystifies and is probably not specific enough for practical use of production people. Actually, there is no general professional understanding of what the term means so far as production is concerned. It could mean a set of small-scale schematics prepared in single-line diagrammatical style. Or it could, and more suitably, mean a comprehensive but incomplete set of drawings: working drawings without the detail and data normally associated with construction drawings.

The latter, General Services Administration (GSA), definition of design development has production of the complete working drawing divided into two phases. First comes the preparation of a drawing in a manner to define and establish the scope of work and design and then, after client approval, comes full development to completion as a working drawing. That interpretation is corroborated by GSA in *Architectural Criteria:* "tentatives Design Development consist of definite double line plans drawn at working drawing scale."

Design development may properly be considered as both a proving-out extension of the initial design effort and the beginning of the production effort, when more and more production expertise, shortcuts, and systems are integrated into drawing production. When the GSA interpretation of design development is employed, there might be a tendency to place too much information on a drawing, before any approvals are obtained or perhaps to place information that is appropriate only to construction. The purpose of design development should not be overlooked. At this particular point, the drawings are principally for the client's information, not for use by any field forces.

One of the advantages of the overlay system is the opportunity to place supplemental information on overlays. That is especially true of schematics and design development. The information is specifically needed by the client to get a thorough understanding of the project. If that information is not needed for working drawings, the overlay containing it can be discarded. Then there will not be the added expense of erasing and redrawing data on the working drawing.

Guide to initial production phases   These, then, are the options available for production of schematics and design development drawings (see also Chapter 5):

1. Prepare schematics in the traditional way: develop on off-size sheets at small scale, single line; discard the drawings after client approval; and begin design development drawings.

2. Prepare design development drawings at working drawing scale on standard-size sheets. Place presentation material on the sheets and then, after client approval, erase all presentation and add data needed for working drawings.

3. Begin all production with the overlay-register technique on standard-size sheets at working drawing scale. Use overlays for special presentation data for both schematics and the design development phase. Reduce the drawings for presentations; discard the overlays; and proceed to working drawings after client approvals. (See Figures 8-1 to 8-3.)

Production technique   Production efficiency rests on standardization and simplification. The overlay-register technique represents uniform standards, and the simplifying of production needs constant attention. The following are some recommendations for simplifying processes:

1. Establish a project manual (Table 5-1).

2. Use sheets of drafting film imprinted with screened grids to avoid having to draw guidelines when doing freehand sketching.

3. Use symbols to identify the materials of partitions and walls rather than place poché directly on plans.

4. Use schedules for repetitive data such as for doors, windows, louvers, finishes, structural elements, and manholes.

5. Avoid the use of complicated codes and symbols to identify building information, which is intended primarily for the worker in the field rather than the drafter.

6. Avoid the use of boxes or outlines around data, notes and dimensions. The boxes may cause confusion in the field.

7. Make match lines stand out clearly, and avoid drawing beyond match lines.

8. Identify detail and section cuts on horizontal plans and vertical elevations. Know where the details apply, and make them easy to find.

9. Provide orderly arrangements of data. For example, head, mullion, and

sill details should be properly grouped and related to each other on the same sheet, not separated.

10. Use established abbreviations consistently. List those used on the sheet where they occur. This is easy to do and is a great help to those in the field.

11. Draw a minimum number of complete building sections. They become expensive to draw. Moreover, they sometimes lose their clarity and often have the least value of all drawing data.

12. Avoid detailing construction systems that are more manufactured than architectural products. Examples are the suspension details of plaster or tile ceilings.

13. Sometimes adding space and area identification to the building elevations of complex structures helps in user orientation.

14. Plan on increasing production proficiency through the use of such proven shortcuts as compositing, cut and paste, appliqués, typewritten notes, standard details, and photodrawing.

Reproducibles   The word "reproducible" refers to a sheet of translucent material upon which an image has been recorded either by hand or by reprographics. Such a sheet is capable of being reproduced or printed by the photographic, diazo, or offset process.

1. A photographic reproducible can be a copy of an original hand-drawn tracing, or it can be a copy of an opaque sheet of material such as a diazo print or a typed sheet. The material of the reproducible will usually be polyester film, which can be smooth on both sides, matte on one side, or matte on both sides. When made directly from an original tracing, a photographic reproducible is usually referred to as a second original or intermediate.

2. A diazo reproducible also can be a copy on polyester film and it can be smooth on both sides or have a matte draftable surface on one or both sides.

3. Reproducibles, or intermediates, are often made on diazo vellum rather than polyester film when the original tracings are vellum or paper and are used in place of the originals for large-volume whiteprinting. Printers will often use them in that way to spare the original paper tracings the beating they would take in numerous runs through the whiteprinter. A diazo copy on vellum paper is also used to make check prints during the course of a project.

Reverse-Read Reproductions   Overlay systems impose rigid standards for registration of all drawings, since imprecise registration jeopardizes the accuracy of image line relations. For that reason, caution must be observed about the use of reverse-read reproductions, in which the image line is recorded on the back side of the sheet and most drafting is to be done on the front side of the sheet. There are times when a reverse-read reproduction is needed, but there is potential for misregistration of the image lines and the registration holes. It may occur if the reprographic technician must turn a negative or a tracing over during contact or photographic project procedures.

SPECIAL PROJECT REQUIREMENTS

Title Sheet Creative architectural ambitions are often dimmed by tedious routines that normally are part of the production of construction documents. The outlets for originality lessen as the project proceeds through elevations, details, schedules, and other production tasks. So the recent graduate wonders about the grandeur of the art of architecture. One place where originality needs rediscovery is the title or cover sheet for the set of construction drawings and specifications. Here the architect can get back in touch with creativity. In magazines and other periodicals there is great emphasis on using artistic talent to put the best face on the publication. Eye-catching magazine covers attract readers; eye-catching cover sheets may attract architectural clients. This is one area where originality is obviously either impressive or unimpressive. The overlay system gives the architect an unexcelled opportunity to use artistic talent in one of the best places for it to be seen: the cover of his own publication, the project set of construction documents (Figure 10-2).

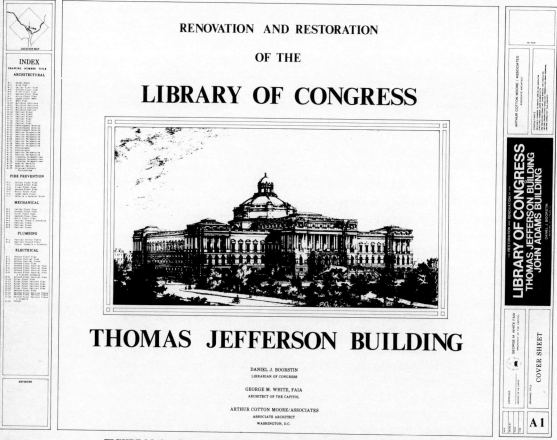

FIGURE 10-2 Cover sheet for a set of architectural drawings. (Arthur Cotton Moore Associates; Robert P. Hammell, AIA, Project Manager)

Project Sign   The title sheet of a set of project drawings can also be used for production of a project sign for use at the site. One approach is to make an englargement of the title sheet, on photographic paper. A photographic reproduction up to 4 by 8 ft. in size can then be plastic-laminated to a sheet of plywood or particle board, mounted on a frame, and installed on the project.

FRAMING GRID AND PLAN TEMPLATE

The first step in plan development is the preparation of a framing grid by either the architect or the structural engineer.

Materials and Tools   Production begins with the two basic components: a standard seven-pin registration bar and 4-mil matte surface polyester drafting film. Before work begins it may be helpful to review fundamentals covered in Chapters 5 and 6.

After preliminary studies and sketches, the grid is hand-drafted, computer-produced, or scribed on a sheet of polyester film. The film can be a blank sheet or a preprinted format sheet with a matte draftable surface on one or both sides. Alternatively, it can be scribe film.

Production Technique   The grid will typically be drawn for the largest plan area of the building. Usually that will be either the ground or the first floor. Priority in the development procedure is to produce the plan that has the greatest impact on progress, the one that has the greatest amount of detail and the greatest input of decisions from management.

Production   Grids can be drawn by hand in pencil or ink, but time and money can be saved by using grids preprinted on drafting film or obtained by computer output. Both types, preprinted or computer-produced, are capable of precise accuracy, are available in a variety of sizes, and are used for floor and ceiling design layouts.

Grids can also be obtained by scribing. The method was described in an article by D. J. Bennett, of Keuffel & Esser Co., in the May 1982 issue of *Plan and Print Magazine:*

> Scribe film is a dry process, fast, correctible and if you scribe at useable plate size, it is your negative, ready for the plate maker. It's also less expensive than the combined use of matte Mylar, pen and ink and film negative. The lines are produced using a scriber with a specific point size to guarantee that a line width won't vary, no matter who does the scribing. All it takes is about two hours of practice.

To produce the plan template, draw in column centerlines, draw the columns to approximate size, and number them. Then draw exterior walls by single line to begin with until problems of design and materials are worked out.

Reproduction   After the grid has been developed into a plan template and is suitable for space planning and structural layouts, reproduction procedures are introduced. The first step is to photograph the template on an 8½- by 11-in negative. The steps that follow differ for multistory projects and single-floor projects only in the number of photocopies to be produced from the reduction negative of the framing grid–plan template, the basis for all procedures. For most multistory projects, photocopies of the framing grid–plan template are produced as follows:

1. For the architect, provide one set of photocopies equal to the number of floors of the project, including basement and roof. All photocopies are to be moist-erasable image line on polyester film, matte one side only.

2. For the structural engineer, provide a set of photocopies like that for the architect, but include the foundation also.

3. Each photocopy of the grid-template becomes an original project tracing that will be worked to completion as an architectural or structural drawing.

4. Since all photocopies are created from the same basic layout, both the architect and structural engineer can get plans into the production process much earlier than if the plans were traced one at a time over the original grid.

5. When the project has a number of similar floors, some judgment must be exercised as to the number of photocopies of the grid-template to be made for the architect and structural engineer. One option is to produce just one copy of the plan template for a typical floor plan development. After space planning for the typical floor is complete, multiple photocopies are made. Each copy then serves as a floor plan base sheet for any one of the floors similar in nature. An alternative is to develop only one floor plan—a typical plan for the similar floors of the project.

6. When deciding upon the method to use, project managers should keep this in mind: If the plan for any floor is likely to be produced at a later stage of the project either by hand or by photocopy, it will cost less to produce it at the working drawing phase, when all elements are geared to production and the actual cost of additional plans may be nothing more than reproduction costs. Providing the sheet or drawing at a later stage in the life of the project, whether by the design professional or a contractor, requires additional expenditures for technical labor and reproduction services.

Benefits of Photocopy Procedures   The technique of using multiple photocopies is a total-system feature. It provides direct and indirect benefits to all team members, benefits that appear repeatedly and usually when needed most during the course of the project. It makes a significant contribution to quality control, coordination, and checking procedures. Because all plans of all floors are produced from the same base plan and by common-pin registry, they will be in precise alignment both vertically and horizontally. The plans of all disciplines—architectural, engineering, and consultant—will match perfectly.

As for control of quality, this method improves efficiency and increases the vcrsatility of coordination and checking. Tracings of architectural drawings are superimposed and checkcd over tracings of other disciplines by using registration bars and light tables. Composite prints also are used for quality control. The tracing of one discipline can be run through a whiteprinter together with any other tracing—for any floor of a project and in any combination needed for coordination and checking—even though the base sheet and overlays may not be printed in that manner for a final issue of drawings.

For example, a structural framing plan can be combined with a plumbing layout and or a duct layout and run through a whiteprinter to get a special print that can provide simple checking for conflicts, errors, and omissions. Although the cost will be minor, costs always have to be taken into account. There is no question of the value of this technique, which can easily become a standard procedure. The savings in time and revisions amount to more up-front savings that help make profit much more secure.

FLOOR PLAN BASE SHEET

The next development step is to carry the plan template to completion as a finished floor plan drawing. The result is a construction drawing, a base sheet the content of which is limited to just construction planning and layout information: columns, exterior walls, interior partitions, doors, windows, stairs, elevators, and mechanical spaces (Figures 10-3 and 10-4).

Developing a space layout can be likened to the actual construction: prepare the plan similarly to the way construction is carried out. Visualizing the construction process during planning is the key to efficient production; it is the way to identify the content of the base sheet. Keeping base sheet content limited to basic construction data enables consultants and engineers to get an early jump on their own work. The policy of minimum sheet content also tends to discourage drafters from using inefficient practices at the drafting board.

Screening Before a decision is made about the number of photocopies to be produced for further development into final drawings, some consideration should be given to screening. Photographic screening has an important application when some floors are set back from floors above or below and others extend out over adjacent levels. When screening is applied to such photocopies, it is usually necessary to do some hand drawing over the screened lines to distinguish clearly between the construction lines that represent various levels. For example, after the hand drawing on the sheet for a setback is complete, the screened lines beyond the perimeter of the layout area will serve as references for the floors below. Because they are screened, the outlines will be clearly indicated as separate from the actual construction lines on the plan.

Screened line strength is another important consideration. Screened lines that are too strong may result in confusing drawings; it may not be easy to tell the difference between construction lines of different levels. On the other

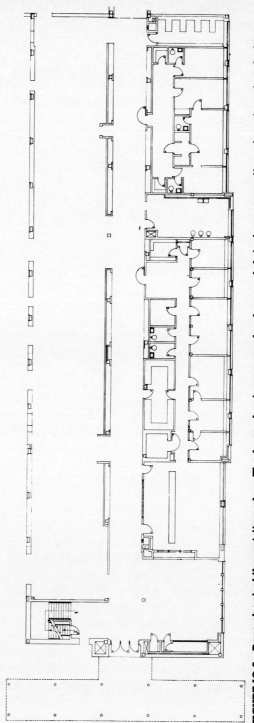

FIGURE 10-3 Base sheet of the existing plan. The base sheet serves as background data for preparation of engineering design. (Jewell, Downing and Associates, Architects, Baltimore, Md.)

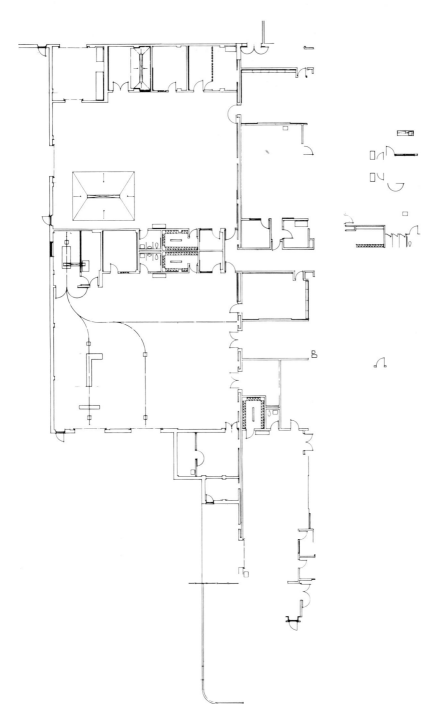

FIGURE 10-4 Base sheet of new-addition plan. The base sheet is a simple line drawing showing basic layout data. Data to size or describe and for construction purposes are placed on overlays. Floor plans are then easier to prepare and read and much more convenient to change. (Jewell, Downing and Associates, Architects, Baltimore, Md.)

hand, although light screened lines may serve the purpose for full-size drawings, lines that are too light may fade out entirely if drawings are reduced for half-size offset printing. Of course, the same thing may happen to hand-drawn lines that are too light to withstand reduction for offset printing. It is helpful to have a number of screen samples on file to guide selections.

General Development Technique   Drawings, of floor plans in particular, are developed on the drafting board through the use of two techniques that are not always apparent to the production team when they are used. They are the continuous and the intermittent methods.

In the continuous method of production, a floor plan is produced by hand drafting in the shortest time and with the fewest interruptions in the hope it will need no change or revision once it is completed to the satisfaction of the project manager or the drafter. Input from consultants and engineers is usually not received until some time after the drawing is complete. The chances are good, therefore, that the eventual input from those members of the team will necessitate changes and revisions.

During production, features of design and space use are proved out and data is fed to the person drawing the plan. This could begin with the design development phase; the drawing would be worked to a point where it would be accepted for that phase. Then work would be resumed on it for the working drawing phase. There would, then, be that one definite interruption before final completion. Project managers tend to favor this technique, as do the drafters, and there are no guidelines to which method should be used for any particular job.

In the intermittent method of production, there is a series of stages of drafting in which only the data that has been proven out is placed on the drawing. At a certain stop point, the drawing is printed for engineers and consultants. Work is then suspended until some input is received from those team members. This method is a more cautious approach to production; the goal is to minimize revisions and redrawing.

Creative design functions and floor plan development are more apt to be team efforts when they are unified and combined by overlay-register techniques. An example is the design of the exterior features of a building. The design studies can be performed simultaneously with space planning. Both the designer and the production drafter are provided with copies of the framing grid and plan template. Each can work on an overlay over a copy of the template; one designer develops features of the building exterior while the other produces interior layouts. The two sheets, when combined with the floor plan base sheet, produce the total plan: interior and exterior features, facades, windows, glazed areas, and materials. All that is produced by team effort and the overlay system.

BID ALTERNATE—BUILDING EXTERIOR

The drawing production method described above can also be used to prepare drawings for bid alternates when it has been decided to price out different materials and/or design features for the building exterior. Bid alternate data is placed on a separate overlay registered with the base sheet. The overlay shows alternate materials, and construction detail would be composited for printing with either the floor plan or the grid-template sheet.

The same method can be applied to other bid alternates: details, plan areas, engineering systems, and so on. Information that applies only to the alternate is placed on the overlay. It is developed over the master base, which is common to both base contract data and bid alternates.

OVERLAY PRODUCTION

The production of architectural overlays is, in general, the same as that of such engineering overlays as site development work.

Materials and Tools Polyester film with a draftable matte surface is required if the overlay is to be hand-drafted. The sheets can be either blank or preprinted formats punched for registration. If the line images are to be produced by appliqué materials—press-on tapes, or other applied graphic materials—smooth sheets are used. The standard seven-pin registration bar is taped down near the top of the drafting board. When extra large drawings are to be made, however, a nine- or eleven-pin registration bar is used.

Drafting Technique The underlay may be either the original base sheet drawing, a photocopy, or a diazo copy. The latter can be produced on a sensitized sheet of polyester film exposed on a vacuum frame flatbed printer and developed in an ammonia process whiteprinter.

The major goal of production, often lost sight of amid the pressures of people problems and technical complications, is to guarantee proper attention to design. The tendency to sacrifice design for drawing productivity has to be recognized, particularly when drafters may be spending their time dressing up drawings with minor and unimportant information. Although the quality of working drawings may impress clients and contractors, there is little value in superfluous information that takes time that would be better spent on design.

The benefits of the overlay drafting system are gained by experience and developed levels of proficiency; they will not be gained automatically. Consequently, instruction should stress the overlay-register technique, basic drafting proficiency, and strong fundamental knowledge of construction methodology. Effective drafting is of little value if what is being drawn cannot be built.

The production of floor plans involves primary elements of information such as dimensions, space titles and numbers, and ceilings. Other data might include schedules, built-in equipment, detail keys, changes in floor levels, and door and window symbols. The arrangement of data on overlays will vary with the type and size of the project and decisions that accord with the needs of consultants. For example, the structural engineer might need overlays for dimensions and room spaces, composited with the floor plan base sheet, to size and locate such elements as columns and floor openings as well as to establish floor loadings. The structural engineer cannot be expected to guess the use of spaces in order to establish floor loading.

Other overlay sheets that might be developed on occasion include flooring patterns, legends, and material indications. Overlay content is determined by needs of consultants and engineers first and only then by architectural needs.

THE DIMENSION OVERLAY

The dimension overlay (Figure 10-5) is prepared on a prepunched sheet of polyester drafting film and is developed over the floor plan base sheet (Figure 10-3). Placing dimensions on a separate sheet rather than on the floor plan itself may appear to be an awkward procedure, but it can be the introduction to more efficient output by all team members. That output includes shop drawings, as-built drawings, building graphics, and future additions and alterations, as well as business development. That is, recording dimensions on a separate sheet is part of a systematic procedure that makes plan develop-ment and dimensioning a much less demanding task and a more orderly process.

When dimensions are placed on overlays, the routine is to begin with the primary ones first. Those are the dimensions that locate and size such elements of the structure as perimeter walls, columns, openings in slabs for vertical transportation, ducts and pipe penetrations, slab depressions, and differences in floor levels.

Further work on the dimension overlay consists of freehand notations of secondary and also unproven dimensions. These are placed directly on the overlay in full knowledge that they are subject to change or proof because they can so easily be changed. Other dimensions can be temporarily placed on a whiteprint of the floor plan. The rough dimensions are continuously formal-ized on the overlay as they are proved out by the completion of various designs and details supplied by engineers and consultants.

Two Dimension Overlays   There are also uses for two separate dimension overlays related to a single floor plan base sheet:

- One overlay contains dimensions common to both architectural and structural drawings.

- One overlay contains dimensions applicable only to design features: furniture, drinking fountains, view windows, movable partitions, and special woodwork.

The use of two overlays aids in coordination of layouts and facilitates the dimensioning of both architectural and structural layouts.

Benefits of Dimension Overlays   The objective in using overlays for dimen-sions is to make dimensioning a relatively minor production effort while helping to minimize changes, erasing chores, and repetitive drafting. Overlays by themselves are much easier to change. Conflicts and errors are easier to

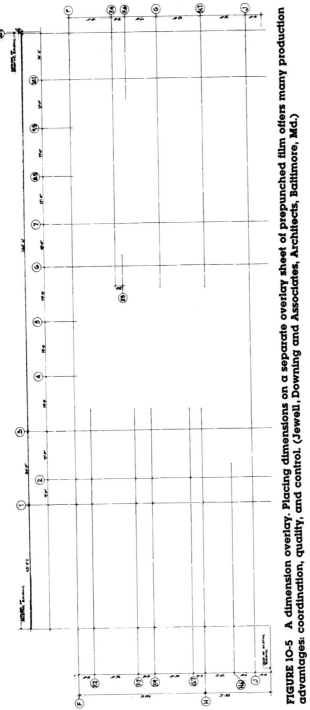

FIGURE 10-5 A dimension overlay. Placing dimensions on a separate overlay sheet of prepunched film offers many production advantages: coordination, quality, and control. (Jewell, Downing and Associates, Architects, Baltimore, Md.)

detect; and when changes must be made, they are confined to dimensions. There is no need to disturb related data, as by erasing it inadvertently and then redrawing it in the same place.

COMPOSITE—THE COMPLETE DRAWING

The conventionally prepared drawing has all the data contained on one sheet in its final form, just as the composite of the overlay-developed production has (Figure 1-5). The advantage of the overlay version lies in the options that ensure closer and easier control of quality, the versatility of dividing information onto different sheets for a variety of reasons, and, normally, reduced production time together with better control of production costs.

To some extent, filing problems also are different. In addition to any project drawings that may have been produced by the conventional method, a composite drawing will have been produced, from base and overlays, by the overlay-register method. The sheets to be filed are a negative, which may be either full size or reduced, and the base sheet and overlays required for production of the negative. If the composite final drawing is photographically produced, it will be of archival quality; if it is a diazo reproduction on polyester film, its archival value may be lower. Research is being done on the production of archival quality diazo reproductions.

Filing of project drawings—base sheets, overlays, and composites—should not become a disproportionate problem. There are a number of recommended methods, but the important factor is organization. As long as a method is selected and employed consistently, filing will not be a major headache. After all, it is esssentially a clerical matter.

NOTES, POCHÉ, AND SYMBOLS OVERLAY

The notes, poché, and symbols overlay is drawn in the same manner as the dimension overlay. Work begins with freehand lettering on either a print of the floor plan base sheet or on a prepunched sheet of polyester film with a draftable matte surface on one side. Alternatively, all data are roughed out on a sheet of sketch paper. Preferably, however, an overlay will be used (Figure 10-6).

This is one sheet that offers unlimited production advantages over conventional drawing methods. Scheduling, coordination, and cost-saving shortcuts go directly on the overlay. Work on this sheet can be suspended while effort is concentrated on design, space planning, and details without affecting the progress of other elements of the project. And while more critical drawings are inactive, as for printing, the sheet can be worked on as a job filler. Holding off on production of the overlay facilitates decisions on the amount and placement of data as well as the shortcut methods to be used during production. The primary concern is the assembly of data rather than hand drafting.

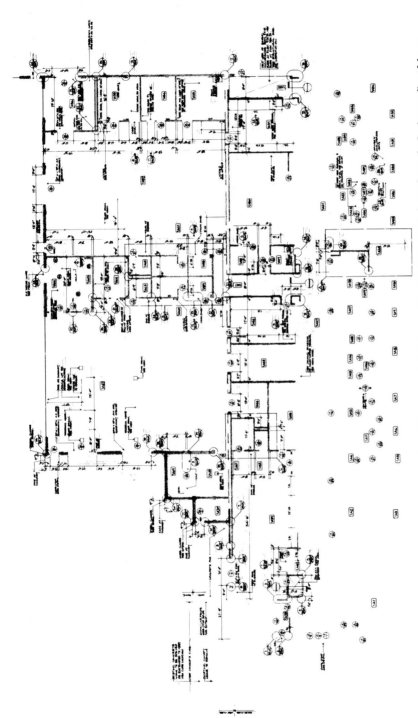

FIGURE 10-6 A notes, poché, and symbols overlay. When special data, such as notes, poché, and symbols, is confined to a separate prepunched overlay sheet, it is easier to change. Basic layout data will not be disturbed unnecessarily when changes must be made. (Jewell, Downing and Associates, Architects, Baltimore, Md.)

Knowing how quickly the sheet can be prepared relieves managers of some pressure. The notes, poché, and symbols overlay is one of the few sheets that can be put together by more than one person at the same time. Particularly when time is running short, production can be broken down into more than one sheet. One sheet might show the space title and number, another the notes and detail references, and a third the schedules. The three could be combined with the floor plan base sheet by compositing.

When all information for the overlay has been collected and the method of producing it has been selected, production of the sheet will be quicker and will cost much less than by conventional drafting methods in conjunction with the floor plan. Any changes in or revisions to the data on the overlay will not affect the data on any related sheet, which might otherwise be in the way of data erasures. Assembly shortcuts include typing on an adhesive-backed sheet, scissors drafting by using such special products as total transfer symbols and reference materials, dry-transfer products for lines, letters, and numbers, and graphic pattern materials for construction information.

Space names and numbers can be furnished to the team members who need them by marking up whiteprints. Alternatively, a quick whiteprint composite can be made of the floor plan base sheet and a quick freehand-noted overlay on a diazo vacuum frame whiteprinter.

CEILING DESIGNS

The design of interior and exterior ceilings, normally called a reflected plan, consists of grid lines with or without a layout of light fixtures (Figure 10-7). The two main considerations in ceiling design are the method of creating the ceiling modules and the variation in size and shape. One room might have a 2- by 4- ft grid in running bond, another in modular style, and a third in 1- by 1- ft grids. Still another room might have a 2- by 4- ft grid running at right angles to other room grids.

Although the apparently desirable production method might be to cut and paste preprinted grids to an overlay sheet of drafting film over various spaces on the floor plan base sheet, the time spent on printing and the numerous cut-and-paste operations might make simple hand-drawing methods advisable. Another cut-and-paste consideration is the printing of the worked overlay, with its pasted-on sheets of grids, for consultants and engineers. A whiteprint with a ghost image of the ceiling plan may be difficult for an engineer to register, and it may be difficult to read or trace over. These problems must be thought out before deciding on the method to be used for producing the reflected plan.

A perfect system would be to have preprinted grids on a prepunched sheet of polyester film with a draftable matte surface upon which related data could be drawn by hand or applied by cut and paste. However, varying room sizes, shapes, and positioning on a plan make such a technique all but impossible. The choices, then, in producing a ceiling grid—and a flooring pattern or paving pattern as well—are pretty much limited to cutting out preprinted grids, and

FIGURE 10-7 The ceiling overlay represents an effective time-saving production technique. All ceiling features, which are often considerable in number, can be coordinated with greater accuracy. (Jewell, Downing and Associates, Architects, Baltimore, Md.)

sticking them in appropriate positions on an overlay sheet or drawing the required grids by hand directly on a prepunched sheet of film.

Ceiling design requires the coordination of architectural and other disciplines concerned with the design, appearance, and construction of ceiling systems:

- *Architectural* Ceiling materials, suspension methods, grid sizes, ceiling breaks and levels, details of openings for vents, access panels, curtain tracks, sliding-door tracks
- *Structural* Sizes and locations of such elements as columns, column caps, beams, and floor-framing members
- *Plumbing* Vertical and horizontal piping, sprinkler systems, and pneumatic tube systems
- *Mechanical* Ceiling grilles and fire-detection units
- *Electrical* Light fixtures and outlets for speakers and communications

Structural Coordination A simple example of structural coordination is to have the engineer place notes to dimension the space remaining, or clearance, between the proposed ceiling and such horizontal structural elements as beams and slabs. The overlay, which would be for information purposes only and would be discarded later, would be composited with either the structural layout of the floor or the architectural floor plan. Whiteprints of the working composite would be distributed to all disciplines for checking their work against potential obstructions.

This is a relatively simple technique that saves the time that other disciplines would spend in hunting for and calculating information that can be readily supplied by the structural engineer. It is an example of how important in the avoidance of problems the volunteering of information can be in the course of a project.

Coordination of Ceiling and Lighting Layout This coordination applies to the ceilings of both interior and exterior spaces. The latter include the undersides of overhangs with plastered surfaces and expansion joints and exterior lighting. A sheet of prepunched polyester drafting film is fitted to the pins of a standard registration bar and superimposed over a copy of or the original floor plan base sheet. The overlay sheet must have at least one draftable matte surface.

The ceiling layout is prepared by either hand drawing or pasting up preprinted grids for all the spaces that get design treatment. After the ceiling design grid layout is complete and has been approved, another prepunched sheet of film is placed over the pins of the registration bar for drawing a light fixture layout. On occasion, time will be saved by sketching freehand until the layout has been reviewed and approved. Then the lighting layout can be formalized on the overlay.

For review and checking, the base sheet and the two overlays can be run through a whiteprinter to obtain a composite blue- or black-line print. The result will be a print with lines and images slightly out of registration, which is usually satisfactory for checking purposes.

After the ceiling and lighting layouts have been approved, the lighting layout is used by the electrical engineer for development of electrical design— circuiting, switching, panels, and so on. The engineer has the option of placing this data directly on the lighting overlay or on another prepunched overlay sheet of drafting film. The preferable option is to show the lighting layout on the ceiling overlay separate from the electrical design. This can be done by compositing or by hand drawing the lighting layout on the ceiling plan.

The system benefits are these:

1. There is less delay between design by the electrical engineer and review and approval by the architect and client. (It is helpful to have light fixture brochures accompany the ceiling and lighting layouts submitted to the client.)

2. The overlay-register technique minimizes the built-in delay factor that often keeps the electrical engineer far behind other project team members. Some effort has to be made to keep that delay to a minimum to facilitate progress and keep changes from getting out of hand.

3. The engineers' drawing responsibilities are lessened; the engineers are spared repetitive work such as drawing plans and erasing and redrawing changes and revisions.

4. Coordination and quality are assured, and output is increased.

5. When a final, complete drawing is issued and the base sheet is screened, the engineering layout is the dominant image. That makes the drawing much clearer and easier to read.

FURNITURE AND FIXTURE PLANS

Details and special plan areas are usually clearer and easier to understand the larger they are drawn, but there are times when drawing at smaller scale is preferred because of the apparent cost advantages. Thorough planning of data placement on a drawing is essential so the drawing will be easily read and understood by those in the field who are responsible for construction. Small-scale details and special plan areas have to be prepared with care to gain the advantages of cost savings while achieving high levels of quality.

Small-scale layouts of furnishings and fixtures can be developed by three possible methods when the drawing is at small scale, say, ⅛ in. The objective is to produce, for construction purposes, a small-scale layout without having to redraw the entire ⅛-in scale floor plan or any part of it. Of the methods described below, one is the overlay type and the other is a modified improvement of the traditional hand-drafted drawing.

Hand-Drafting Method A modification of the traditional hand-drawing method has some potential for saving time and cost over the all-hand-drafted method.

1. After the floor plan base sheet is complete enough for printing purposes, it is photocopied on moist-erasable polyester film. The copy does not have to be a system-registered base sheet. The photoreproducible can be either screened or full-strength line or reverse-read with the image line on the back side of the sheet.

2. Now all that is needed is to hand-draw the furniture and fixture layout directly on the front side of the sheet. When it is complete, the drawing becomes an original and included in the project set of drawings.

The main disadvantage of this method arises from the problem of quality. Changes in and revisions to the floor plan, as well as to the furniture and fixture layout, have to be made to keep the drawing up to date. Also, there are likely to be conflicts of information; notes and dimensions on the original floor plan may be obscured by added data such as furniture. To some extent this can be minimized by screening the background data, the floor plan.

Overlay Method   The second method is a modified version of the overlay-register technique in which all sheets are punched and registered during production. Significant gains in time and cost savings are to be realized with this method.

First, a normal, full-size copy of the floor plan base sheet is produced. The copy can be either:

▪ A *photoreproducible* reverse-read image line on the back side of the sheet (the smooth base). There should be a draftable matte surface on the front side. The reproduction should be moist-erasable line, which can be either full strength or screened at the architect's option.

▪ A *diazo-reproducible* reverse-read erasable-line image on the smooth side of the sheet with a draftable matte surface on the front side. Again, full or screened line strength is the architect's option.

Although either a photographic copy or a diazo copy can be used, the diazo copy will cost less.

A furniture and fixture layout is drawn directly on the matte surface side of the punched and registered copy of the floor plan base sheet. In this production step the background data is actually the image line on the back of the sheet rather than a registered copy pinned to a registration bar. In other words the copy and the overlay are worked together as one sheet, the plan on the back and the overlay data on the front. Freehand sketching of the furniture and fixture layout to begin with can help minimize changes in the final drawing. The layout is formalized after approval.

Changes and revisions   During the development of the project, changes involving both the floor plan base sheet image line on the back of the sheet and the lines hand-drawn on the front of the sheet, in pen or ink, are likely to occur. When changes are to be made in the original floor plan tracing, the architect has two options. One is to erase the work to be changed on the back of what is now a copy-overlay and then redraw the corrections by hand in pencil or ink. The second is to just erase and not redraw any part of the floor plan, leaving the erased space empty on the back of the sheet.

Since changes will already have been made on the original floor plan base sheet, there is really no need to draw that same changed information on the copy-overlay; the two sheets are already in registration with each other. When the two sheets are eventually composited together as a final drawing, the original floor plan base sheet will provide all the missing floor plan information.

Changing the furniture and fixtures layout Changes in the furniture and fixtures layout can be made on the front side of the sheet, where the layout has been drawn in pencil or ink. First the areas to be changed are erased, and then they are redrawn in the conventional way. Either the original base sheet tracing is placed on a registration bar and the furniture and fixture layout is superimposed on it by fixing it to the pins of the bar or a tracing is made over a revised whiteprint of the floor plan. The first is the usual procedure, and there may be some loss of registration by the second procedure.

Blank spaces After a number of plan changes have been made on the back of the sheet and no corrections have been drawn, there will be a number of blank spaces on the floor plan side of the sheet. That will not present a problem during final compositing, since the sheet is in registration with the original floor plan base sheet. The appearance of the copy-overlay sheet will be a little unusual—as though it has an incomplete floor plan. On occasion it may be advisable to erase the entire floor plan on the back side of the sheet and leave the overlay with only the hand-drawn layout on the front side. That is another of the architect's options. It may be a necessary one when there is some possible conflict of floor plan data because some changes were not picked up and actually made on the plan recorded on the sheet.

Advantages of the method The method offers these advantages:

1. Since the overlay is created on a copy of the base sheet, there is a savings in the cost of the sheet; it does not have to be a slick throwaway after production is complete. Even when a diazo copy is used, there will be no problem about archival quality because the diazo lines have no impact on the final overlay.

2. There are fewer sheets to handle and place on the registration bar, and, of course, this method can be applied to all other production activities of engineers and consultants.

3. When plan changes are made, there is no need to issue new slick throwaways. This is a cost savings to weigh against the cost of erasing plan changes on the back of the overlay sheet.

CHAPTER ELEVEN

Alterations and Additions

This chapter describes the use of the overlay system when an existing structure is to be altered or added to. Such a project presents unusual and complicated design and drawing production problems. There is always a need for a better way to put together a thoroughly and efficiently prepared set of project drawings. Some of the objectives of the overlay system when applied to alteration and addition projects are the following:

- To reduce contractors' claims for job extras
- To reduce the owner's and the architect's liability risks as much as possible by providing drawings with improved readability and accuracy
- To make best use of effective, well-known production shortcuts involving photography, graphic arts materials, scissors drafting, photodrafting, and reuse of existing record information

BASE SHEET DEVELOPMENT

Most of the methodology described in this chapter has to do with the production of base sheets for use in the development of overlays with which final drawings are made. The four methods that are examined in detail offer different ways to develop basic base sheet data from existing building data when changes in the existing data must be made before any production work can begin. They are as follows:

- Changing by photography, or reprographics
- Changing by hand erasing and redrawing
- Changing by scissors drafting and assembly
- Production without any changes made to the original copy

Reprographics Method The reprographics method, and also the other methods, makes use of records of the existing structure. The records may be original tracings on paper, linen, or polyester film or prints. Efforts to locate any building records will be worthwhile, no matter whether the prints are blue or white and no matter what their condition may be. Even prints of the poorest condition can be reclaimed by reprographics creative artistry for use in projects involving additions or alterations. By varying exposure time, opaquing, and masking, a damaged print or record can be transformed into a high-quality "original" tracing on polyester film. This is a very high level professional service, and architects should become thoroughly acquainted with it.

The reprographic method of producing an elementary form of base sheet can result in either a full-size or a reduction negative. Use of a process camera-projector unit to produce an 8½- by 11-in negative is preferred because of the lower negative cost. Less correction work is required, and the product is much higher in quality because of the versatility of the restoration process. Note that if the original drawings were processed on a camera-projector unit, a reduction negative for the project will be on file.

After the existing work is recorded on an 8½- by 11-in negative, necessary corrections are made by masking, blocking out with opaquing fluid, and/or other restoration techniques. This work is usually done at the reprographics facility, but it can be done at the office of the design professional if the facilities, equipment, materials, and know-how are available. Some of the corrections that may be made include sheet borders, title block data, schedules and notes, dimensions, and construction data.

When all the corrections and changes have been made on it, the original image is again recorded by photography and then projected onto a full-size punched sheet of polyester film with a moist-erasable image and a matte drafting surface on one side. The resulting sheet product is the new, but unfinished, original. It is at proper scale, but it lacks all the new work to be performed in the addition or alteration project. The punched sheet now serves as a base sheet. After drafting on it is complete, it will be used for the development of overlays in accordance with standard system requirements.

The placement of elementary data, such as existing floor plan layouts, on the new original should be planned to accommodate additional data to be placed on the sheet by hand drawing or by photographic compositing. Examples are border lines, title blocks, schedules, and notes. Screening is another important factor. For example, existing conditions that are to remain might be screened so the hand-drawn lines will stand out.

Demolition work can be shown in a number of different ways:

1. By preparing a separate overlay, registered to the base sheet, on a sheet of polyester film with a matte surface on one side.

2. By drawing directly on the new photoreproducible original. Existing material to be removed is shown by broken lines.

3. By using appliqué materials such as press-on tape to indicate material to be removed. The material is placed either on the base sheet original or on an overlay sheet. Uses of press-on tape include the indication of fire ratings for walls and partitions.

Hand Work Upgrading a copy of an original drawing by hand obviously requires a copy of the original. This can be obtained by either full-size negative photography or by reduction negative photography with a camera-projector. The photoreproducible should be of the moist-erasable-image type on polyester film punched for registration. The sheet should have a draftable matte surface on one side so that, after all hand erasing of unnecessary information, the new data can be drawn back on the sheet in either pencil or ink. Data to be drawn on the sheet will be that needed to make the sheet serve as a base sheet for the preparation of architectural, structural, plumbing, mechanical, and electrical overlays.

Assembly Methods. The term "assembly" refers to such production shortcuts as application of graphic arts materials, cut and paste, and scissors drafting. The goal is to produce, with minimal hand work, a complete floor plan base sheet original for subsequent preparation of system overlays.

First obtain a whiteprint of the original drawing of the existing building if one is available. Next, cut out the entire area of unneeded and unwanted information, in one or more pieces, and tape or paste the remainder of the print to a sheet of punched polyester drafting film. The patched-together sheet is then photographically reproduced by a camera-projector unit onto a sheet of polyester film with a moist-erasable image and a draftable matte surface. In part, this will be a restoration job, since there is likely to be a need to strengthen some lines in addition to performing some opaquing and masking during the processing of the reduction negative.

An alternative is to use the original tracing of the existing structure. The information on the tracing that will not be needed on the new project can be masked out by cutting a piece of paper and taping it to the tracing. After the masking or scissors work is complete, the patched-together sheet is photographed and recorded on a sheet of prepunched polyester film with a moist-erasable image and a draftable matte surface on one side.

Another way to accomplish the same thing is to have the work done by the reprographics facility. A print of the plan to be altered is marked to show the material to be removed. The plan area is then masked out on the drawing pinned to the vertical copyboard. After a negative is made, the original tracing of the existing building is returned to the file.

Projection photography for these methods requires precision photographic equipment and vertical copyboards with front and back lighting to minimize defects that are involved with the scissors drafting technique (Figure 6-5).

Original Data Use   In production without changes made to the original copy, a minimum amount of hand and photographic modification is involved. This method is probably the easiest and most economical to apply in some projects. Again, an original tracing or a print of the existing structure will be needed. The record, whichever it is, will be taken through photographic procedures to obtain a photoreproducible with a moist-erasable image line and a draftable matte surface. Photography can be either by the full-size or process camera-projector technique.

The reproducible, the elementary new original, is turned over to a drafter for development of a new floor plan design of the changed work. Lines hand-drawn with either pencil or ink will run right through and over lighter lines if the latter are screened on the new original. The screened lines will indicate either existing work to remain or, in association with hand-drawn lines, existing work to be removed. In other words, there will be contrasts of light screened and heavier hand-drawn lines that will indicate new construction.

An alternative is to draw all proposed work on an overlay rather than directly on the photoreproducible—the new original. After the proposed work is drawn to the extent of base sheet definition, a new base sheet is in hand. A composite of the copy of the corrected original record drawing and the manually prepared overlay showing new work will be an intermediate for the development of all other project drawings. This intermediate can be produced on clear-base polyester film, and the background data can be screened. An advantage of this procedure is that any changes to the plan for new work will not affect the image on the original drawing. Whenever any significant changes take place, a new composite intermediate can be obtained. Another advantage of the technique is that screen strength can be changed to conform to quality demands. For example, the plan can be screened and new work shown in full-line strength. Still other advantages are savings effected by avoiding the labor of corrective work: erasing, opaquing of negatives, and masking out data.

When this method is used, there will be occasional need for notes to explain conflicts that may not be too clear to the builder. The conflicts may make existing building features that are to be removed appear to be features that are to remain. But it will be economically more desirable to use notes on such occasions than to make deletions from the drawing.

CHAPTER TWELVE

Details and Special Areas

The overlay system can be usefully employed to explain and clarify important and complex features of a design project. This chapter covers that use of the overlay system in the development of enlarged details and special plan areas such as kitchens, medical facilities, and assembly rooms.

Generally, construction and assembly features and difficult plan functions are pictured at small scale, such as ⅛ in. As the details become more complex, the chances for misunderstandings in the field increase. If the designer is to have confidence that completed work will match design intent, the production personnel must resort to enlargement techniques to clearly delineate construction features that may be difficult for field forces to interpret. Another reason for enlarging such features is to make it easier to evaluate both construction difficulties and cost. The clearer the picture, the better the chances for high-quality work at the least expense.

PLANS FOR SPECIAL LAYOUTS

Base Sheet Development A large-scale layout, or blowup, has characteristics identical with those of the primary small-scale layout except that, obviously, the information shown on the large-scale detail sheet covers less plan area. Now, the process of converting small-scale plan and detail data into larger, easier-to-understand graphics can be either a totally hand production effort or a mechanically assisted function employing precision photographic technology. Both methods, in effect, are a means of changing scale. The two different production methods applied to development of large-scale plan areas are as follows:

Hand production   No matter how proficient or skillful the drafter might be, errors and omissions are almost certain to occur during the slow, costly process of transferring data from one sheet to another and changing the scale. The manual procedure typically starts with a punched sheet of polyester drafting film, matte surface on one side. A preprinted format sheet might be considered for development of the base sheet. On this sheet, by using a manual scale-changing technique, all layout data for a particular area or areas of a plan is sufficiently developed to be suitable for the production of overlays for ceiling design, dimensions, schedules, notes, and engineering data.

Reprographic production   The advantage of the reprographic technique for the development of large-scale layouts and details is not just speed of production but also accuracy. The photographic equipment that is used preserves the quality already there, and it is precisely accurate.

The choice between hand and reprographic production is based on cost, time factors, and perhaps the intention to do offset printing in color. When there is a shortage of work, hand production may be the way to go; when the drafting staff is overloaded, it is an advantage to know how to use reprographics in the production effort.

As with other techniques, efficient production reflects skillful planning. To prepare for the reprographic production of a base sheet, first mark a white-print of the small-scale floor plan to indicate the area to be enlarged. The location of the detail on the new drawing, having been established, must then be made known to the reprographic specialist either by written instructions or by preparing a simple sheet model.

Vital to sheet model planning is calculating the amount of space a detail drawn originally to a small scale will require when transferred to another drawing at a larger scale. It is easy to underestimate the space a plan detail such as a large kitchen–dining room or a medical facility will require. Careful planning of the sheet model will reveal whether a plan area, when enlarged, will require two match-lined sheets instead of just one sheet.

Next, the sheet model showing the position of the detail plan on the new drawing and the whiteprint showing the area to be reproduced at large scale are sent to the reprographic specialist. Also sent will be the original tracing of the primary floor plan or, if one was produced earlier for some other purpose, a reduction negative 8½- by 11-in in size. Otherwise, the original tracing is mounted on the vertical copyboard and photographed to obtain a negative. Afterward the tracing is removed from the copyboard and filed and the negative is removed from the camera, processed, and masked so only the area of the original drawing to be reproduced is exposed for projection.

Finally, a full-size sheet of photosensitive film, punched for registration, is mounted on the copyboard and the new negative is mounted in the camera-projector unit. Before projection takes place, the reprographic specialist, having consulted the sheet model prepared by the architect, arranges the sheet of film on the copyboard so the projected image will fall in a position that matches the one shown on the sheet model. The selected image is then projected onto the sheet with the projector set for scale changing, say, from ⅛ in of the original tracing to ¼ in of the new detail. The result is a new original, a detail sheet suitable as a base sheet for further overlay production.

Overlays for Detail Plans As a rule, overlays will be produced for detail plans in the same manner as, for example, overlays for floor plans. They will involve such data as dimensions, ceiling layouts, furniture and fixtures, plumbing, mechanical, electrical, communication, and sprinkler systems.

Composites The final complete detail plan sheets are composited together with appropriate overlay sheets to produce drawings corresponding to conventionally prepared drawings (Chapter 7).

Scale Changing Information drawn by hand on the primary small-scale plan should be accurate and have sharp, thin, consistent line strength. Avoid lines that, when enlarged, become excessively dark and heavy or are too light and require additional hand work to correct line values after photographic enlargement.

The production technique to be used should be selected early. Consider such questions as these: How much work should be performed on the basic small-scale plan before work is started on detail plan sheets? Should details be proved out first at large scale and then drawn on the small-scale plan? Whatever the production method employed, some drafters will find it useful to merely profile the area on a small-scale plan that is to be duplicated at larger scale on another detail drawing.

VERTICAL TRANSPORTATION

Base Sheet Development The normal complexity of the vertical transportation elements of a project dictate the need for large-scale, easier-to-understand details such as ¼-in scale plans and vertical sections cut through walls, doors, and penthouse machine rooms above roof lines. When the overlay technique is to be used, base sheet development is the same for different plan elements such as stairs, elevators, and conveyors.

Elevators are installed by shop drawings, but the architect's design contributions include car size and capacity and the location and size of wall and floor openings, shafts, and machine rooms. Although shop drawings are used for elevator installation, the architect must work out clearances between cars, walls, and beams to be certain the car size and structural elements within the shaft fit the available space.

As for the plans for special layouts discussed earlier in this chapter, the two production methods for vertical transportation detailing are hand and reprographic.

Multiple Detail Procedure The details of vertical transportation usually require that more than one plan be shown—a typical floor plan plus pit and machine room plans. The latter may include adjacent areas such as utility rooms and ductwork shafts. When a number of plans must be placed on one sheet, use is made of a multiple-exposure technique at the reprographics facility. The process camera-projector unit shown in Figure 6-6 is used. The architect furnishes the following materials needed for this technique:

- A whiteprint of the small-scale floor plan marked with crayon or ink to show the precise area of the plan to be reproduced.

- The original tracing of the plan or a small-size negative if one is available.

- A sheet model showing the positions of the various plans to be reproduced at large scale on a new original drawing that is to be produced by reprographics. This positioning sheet can be prepared freehand, since there is seldom a need for precise layout accuracy. The reprographics specialist does, however, use all available means, such as grid lines, columns, walls, and partitions, to get elements aligned.

The elevator and/or stair core plans shown on a detail sheet may include a plan for each floor of a project if there are significant differences between floors or perhaps just three plans: pit, typical, and machine room. Whatever the number of plans to be placed on a sheet that will become a final project drawing, a skillfully prepared sheet model will enable the reprographic specialist to use precision technical resources to produce a drawing requiring a minimum of drafting time and expense to complete. Each of the photographically produced layouts will be derived from the same data, either a typical plan or a plan containing basic data common to either all or most elevator floor layouts including grid lines, columns, beams, partitions, walls, floor openings, and elevator cars. Obviously, the locations of elements of vertical transportation should be fixed before any detail development takes place.

Reprographic procedures Follow the directions given under "Reprographic production" except for the projection procedures (blowback). Before blowback takes place, the following procedure is employed. It is a kind of step-and-repeat process, and it is performed under darkroom conditions.

1. As many registration bars as might be needed are mounted on the vertical copyboard. They are installed close together, straight and level.

2. A full-size sheet, prepunched for registry, is pinned and taped for security to one pin bar. This will be polyester photosensitized film, matte drafting surface one side. The image will be right side up. The positions of the registration bars and the sheet pinned to the bar will be determined by the sheet mock-up provided by the architect. This sheet mock-up shows the positions of the detail plans on the new original drawing to be produced by reprographic techniques.

3. Next, multiple projection takes place. That is, the masked image on the negative is projected back onto the sensitized sheet as many times as required

and in the positions shown on the sheet mock-up. Since the projector is fixed in position both laterally and vertically, it is the sheet on the copyboard that must be moved for multiple image recording. The camera operator estimates the amount of movement needed to get the sheet in position for each of the projection steps that take place in order to get all the needed images recorded on the sheet. The scale of each detail plan is also determined with precision by the technician. Hand drafting to complete the drawing involves changes from a typical floor plan to the special features of a pit plan and those of the machine room.

The step-and-repeat procedure works well when one image, isolated on a negative by masking, is projected a number of times horizontally across a sheet. When the architect wishes to have additional lineups of identical or similar detail plans on the same sheet, accuracy is not quite so easy to achieve, particularly when it is important to have layouts line up vertically so far as grids, columns, partitions, and walls are concerned. Then the camera technician must use the eyeball technique to gain accurate vertical alignment. That technique is used, however, only with the architect's knowledge and consent.

To obtain a double lineup—two or more horizontal setups of details on one sheet, all derived from one particular plan area on one key drawing such as a primary floor plan—a previously recorded negative is masked to isolate the area to be recorded, enlarged, and positioned on a new sheet as an original project drawing.

After the negative is masked and placed in the camera-projector unit, the isolated image is momentarily projected onto the copyboard so the technician can spot the approximate location in which the new detail will appear so the sheet of reproduction film can be positioned to receive the detail image. The camera-projector unit is reset at this time so the operator can check the accuracy of the scale.

Now a prepunched sheet of photosensitive film is mounted on pins on the copyboard so the projected detail image will appear in the position shown on the architect's sheet mock-up. After the sheet has been positioned properly on the pins, a strip of masking tape is placed vertically on the copyboard alongside one edge of the sheet to mark the starting point for all movement of the sheet as individual images are recorded. The camera technician might also mark the starting position on the pins of the registration bar, so the masking tape will be an insurance measure. Next, through a series of image projections and lateral sheet movements, the detail is recorded as many times as shown on the sheet mock-up to complete one horizontal lineup of details.

To start recording the second lineup, either above or under the first lineup, the technician merely moves the pin bars up (or down) with the sheet attached, reattaches the bar and sheet to the copyboard, and begins shooting images onto the sheet until a second horizontal lineup is achieved. By using a combination of masking tape for vertical matching point alignment and one or more registry bars for horizontal alignment, an accurate layout of a series of similar details can be produced photographically and economically.

Alternative methods The reprographic technique provides the architect with a precision, sophisticated production method. However, the same result can also be reached by scissors drafting and pasteup, and sometimes at less cost and in less time.

Completion Procedures The semicomplete detail sheet produced by the step-and-repeat process can be worked to completion either by conventional hand drafting or through the use of overlays. The main disadvantage to handwork is the need for all disciplines involved to keep their own versions of the sheet up to date. If engineers are to produce layouts in conjunction with the detail sheet, they must be provided with either diazo reproductions for use as base sheets or photoreproductions with draftable matte surface.

Overlay production By using the photographically produced detail drawing, with either one or two rows of layouts, as a base sheet, overlays will be produced for such data as dimensions, ceiling plans, space labels, notes, and material indications.

VERTICAL TRANSPORTATION DETAILS

Base Sheets The base sheet for vertical transportation details at large scale, the primary element of the total drawing, will usually be prepared by hand, but development by computer output can be expected in the near future. Details will be developed as usual on prepunched sheets of 4-mil polyester drafting film with a matte drafting surface one side. Preprinted format sheets might also be considered for this purpose.

Production technique The architect usually provides the basic layout for the base sheet showing floor levels, shaft size, partitions, walls, and approximate size of structural elements. Once the sheet is blocked out with this data, it is turned over to the structural engineer for sizing beams, slabs, and columns. Checks are made for clearances over doors.

When the architectural and structural development work has been done, the sheet is reproduced. A diazo copy is made for use by either the structural engineer or the architect depending upon whose work might be considered dominant for the development of detail data. Since it is unlikely that the original base sheet will be complete at this stage, the combined architectural and structural drawing should be developed to completion. Information and details are added as they are proved out by the responsible design team members.

Overlays The vertical transportation overlay sheets include those for horizontal and vertical dimensions, material indications, and notes and labels.

Composites The complete working drawing in its final, formal issue is the composite prepared in typical overlay fashion.

Advantages of Overlay Technique for Details Overlay techniques for composing details cannot be considered standard because there is no such thing as a standard project. Special coverage of the techniques is provided here to acquaint the design professional with their potential, but their costs must be evaluated. When there are positive opportunities for employing overlay techniques for details, the following advantages are usually available:

1. Each discipline involved has access to certain information that was drawn only once: basic detail layout data, vertical and horizontal dimensions, floor level data, and space labels.

2. Normally, duplication of effort is eliminated and coordination is improved. Preparation of identical details, often at different scales, is eliminated. For example, architectural interest in elevators is limited to design features. Other vital data is of a structural nature or is in the special province of the equipment manufacturer, so there is less need for it to appear on any architectural drawing.

3. Overlays also have the attractive potential for final printing in color. Certain detail features can be highlighted to make drawings clearer, easier to read, and more interesting to those who use them for construction purposes.

4. Visual coordination is facilitated by overlay methods. Drawings of base sheets and overlays of various disciplines can be pin-registered over one another for checking, simplifying the process, and exposing critical errors before they become expensive mistakes during construction.

CONSTRUCTION AND ASSEMBLY DETAILS OF WALL SECTIONS

Construction and assembly details are technical problems less than they are design problems. Two vital factors are involved in effective solutions:

1. Mastery of the product, that is, a design professional's knowledge of basic construction methods and materials to ensure that details presented on construction drawings are buildable.

2. Skill in building the detail, that is, visualizing and placing components together and assembling them on the drawing in the same manner they will be built.

Those abilities are not easily acquired; consequently, a hand-drawn unbuildable detail on an architectural drawing will occasionally be rebuilt in the field. When that happens, it will often incur extra expense to the client or project owner. It may also differ somewhat from the original design intent. In most projects the amount of detail drafting time that can be afforded is weighed against the amount of detail needed for proper and economical construction that meets design objectives. The amount of detail shown can easily become largely wasted effort—a matter of repetition and unnecessary information perhaps drawn just to keep someone busy. Such factors erode drafting room productivity.

But although the amount of detail on a drawing should be minimized to save money or must be minimized because there is a lack of drafting skill and proficiency, it is still necessary for field forces to have something to guide their construction of details. In the course of the project, the design staff is constantly confronted with the need to produce high-level professional detail with a minimum effort and by use of contemporary drafting practices and effective tools. The overlay system can be particularly effective in production of complex details in conjunction with professional knowledge of construction practices. Two detail production features are discussed: wall sections for new construction and wall section details for additions to existing structures.

Wall Details for New Construction

Base sheet production   Creating the base sheet by scissors drafting and pasteup is an effective time-saving method, particularly when the project is complex and has a number of different wall sections. Production starts on a sheet of 4-mil polyester drafting film punched for registry. For a large project there will be a number of sheets with wall section details to a scale of, say, ½ in or larger. On this work sheet a number of different wall sections are profiled with different meanings in reference to materials—masonry, metal, glass, or any combination. In profiling, construction features are outlined, but minus such particular data as dimensions, notes, and materials.

When the profiles are satisfactory, the sheet is reproduced by the diazo process either in-house, if the capability is present, or by a reprographic plant. The number of copies needed will equal the number of wall sections to be placed on separate sheets to become final project drawings. The number of copies made for scissors drafting purposes will also take into account the nature of the wall, openings for windows and doors, louvers, waterproofing, and building connections. Screening might be considered for copies made on diazo film, since the final drawing data will stand out more clearly on screened copies.

After the original tracing and the diazo copies are returned to the drafting room, each separate wall section profile is cut out of the diazo sheet it is on and pasted onto a sheet of polyester drafting film punched for registry. Format sheets might be considered for this purpose. After the cutout wall section profiles are pasted up on sheets of drafting film, hand drafting is used to add information needed to complete the working drawing. In fitting individual details to the pasteup sheet, the details are aligned both vertically and horizontally to match floor levels, heads of openings, and coursing.

The base sheet or sheets can be completed by hand drafting directly on the pasteup sheet or on a photoreproduction of it. It is usually easier to work on a photoreproduction—a new sheet of drafting material—rather than on a sheet with pasted-on pieces of drawings.

Overlays for New Construction Wall Sections   Typically, the information to be placed on overlays for new construction wall sections is the same as that shown on other overlays. The prepunched sheets will contain assembly and connection details, notes, references, material indications, title, and engineering data. How such information is separated for placement on individual base sheets and overlays is determined by such factors as size and complexity of detail, use of screening, and offset printing in multicolors.

Overlay options   In addition to the normal applications of overlays, the design team may expedite drafting production by using overlays for joint preparation of detail when there is more than one source of data. An example is a wall section with both architectural and structural features. The common development of layout, assembly, connections, and materials can often lessen the chance of errors and omissions and make checking and coordination easier for team members to accomplish.

Another factor that is easily overlooked is the constructor's vital interest in building an entire detail from one picturization rather than from details scattered throughout the project set of drawings. The scattered details are not always easy to find, and they can be expensive to build. It may not always be practical or even possible to combine data from different disciplines into one complete detail, but it is in the best interests of efficient, least-cost construction to concentrate information as much as possible.

ALTERATION AND ADDITION DETAILS

Base Sheet Production   In the normal fashion, base sheets for alteration and addition details are prepared on prepunched 4-mil polyester drafting film with a matte surface. Either a single- or two-sheet method can be used. In the single-sheet method, all data on both existing conditions and proposed work is placed on one sheet. In the two-sheet method, data on the existing construction is placed on one sheet and data on the proposed work is placed on a separate sheet. The choice of method is related to decisions on the use of screening to tone down data having to do with the existing structure and the possibility of multicolor offset printing. The more base and overlay sheets are employed during production, the more options there will be for visual emphasis on different aspects of detail.

Two-sheet method   The information needed for the preparation of a base sheet showing existing conditions includes one or more of the following:

- Original tracings
- Prints of original tracings that can be turned into second originals by photo restoration
- Drawings made by field measurements of existing conditions
- For certain projects, base sheets made entirely of photos of existing conditions

Original tracings are preferred, but they are usually unavailable; then the second choice is prints of originals. The effort to find and restore original documents, no matter what condition they may be in, is always worthwhile. If the original tracing is available but cannot be used as a base sheet, a photoreproduction on draftable matte surface can be made. Some masking or opaquing to remove title block data, borders, dimensions, unrelated notes, and references will usually be required. Prints, if they are in good condition, can be scissors-drafted. Usable information is cut out of the prints and pasted or taped to a prepunched sheet of polyester drafting film.

The base sheet for new work is prepared in the usual manner to show the relation of the proposed work to the existing conditions. That includes structure to remain undisturbed as well as that to be changed or removed. The drafting involved is done on a sheet superimposed by register pins over the base sheet that shows existing conditions. That makes it possible to screen or tone down the images representing existing conditions in order for the new work to stand out. This technique also makes possible offset printing in different colors.

Single-sheet method. A single sheet that shows both the existing conditions and the new work can be composed by all hand drafting. The original data is transferred to the new sheet by hand work, and to it is added, by hand drafting, all the new work. An alternative is to use photoreproduction in part. The original tracing, or a print, of the existing conditions is printed full-line strength or screened on a prepunched sheet of photosensitive polyester film with a matte draftable surface one side. All new work is then added to the sheet by conventional hand drafting.

Overlays Information shown on overlays, prepared in typical system manner, will include such data as connection details, dimensions, material indications, engineering data, and catalog data.

Composites The final detail drawing produced by combining a base sheet and overlays will be the equal in quality of the conventionally hand-prepared drawing. Plus that, it will have the potential for screening and multicolor printing to add clarity and interest.

Use of Photos of Existing Conditions Production versatility should include proficiency in the use of photographs not only to show existing conditions but, in some instances, to show new work, particularly site development. A base sheet full of photographs can become a valuable production asset when it is combined with an overlay sheet to identify special features or work that might be difficult to illustrate in the conventional manner or to understand. The overlay could become the screened element of the final composite.

CHAPTER THIRTEEN

Engineering Design with Overlays

This chapter discusses how the overlay system influences the outcome and output of engineering designs. The engineer must rely on architectural data but has little reason to copy exactly the plans and details that the architect puts on paper, linen, or film. The engineer's primary interest is in transposing calculations into graphic interpretations and system designs. Therefore, redoing either the architect's drawing or the changes the architect makes in plans and details during the course of the project is an outdated way to perform engineering services. The overlay system makes possible the elimination of unnecessary effort from the production of essentials and increases emphasis on design. The basic aspects of the system are summarized here. For a fuller treatment, see Chapter 7.

The architectural base sheet, usually a floor plan, may be composed by hand or be a pasteup, but the engineer need not know which method is used. He or she works only with a copy of that base sheet, usually a diazo copy. This is the formal documentation of layout data upon which engineering design is based. Therefore, the usual policy is to make the copy for the single purpose of developing overlays that show only engineering systems. The copy is made on polyester film to ensure sheet stability; it is punched for registration to guarantee alignment of images on different sheets; it is devoid of matte surfacing to prevent unauthorized hand drafting; and it is usually reproduced with a fixed line image to discourage any changes to it that may make it differ from the original. The copy has only temporary value and will eventually be discarded.

The alternative to the throwaway copy is the reverse-read copy, on which the engineer can make any changes that are sent to him by the architect. This alternative, described in Chapter 10, allows architectural or engineering drafting personnel to make erasures in the copy to agree with changes made in the original base sheet. The reverse-read reproduction can be either a photore-production or a copy made on diazo-sensitized film, which has a moist-erasable image on its reverse side. All hand drafting then takes place on the front side in either pencil or ink.

The changes in the original base sheet are transmitted by full- or small-size prints, depending on the extent of changes. The drafter then erases the void work on the back of the reverse-read copy, places the revised detail or plan underneath the copy, and changes the data on the copy. It is not necessary to draw in base sheet or background data, since that has already been recorded on the original architectural tracing. The engineer needs to be acquainted with this technique. It is an alternative to the standard overlay system technique, and the decision to use it is part of project planning. The following are points to observe.

- Sheets should be worked on in the flat position rather than rolling them at the bottom of the board.

- Check sheets for proper fit on registration bars; sheets that are loose on the pins will tend to get out of registration. Have the sheets repunched if any holes do not line up with the pins.

- Before drawing on overlay sheets, confirm that architectural base sheets are sufficiently developed that overlay drafting will not have to be redone if major modifications are made to base sheets. Also confirm that the base sheet does not contain an excessive amount of data that will conflict with or obscure critical engineering data when composites are produced.

- Retain all copies of base sheets until the project has been printed for bidding. Make certain that composites are produced only from up-to-date base sheets and overlays.

STRUCTURAL DESIGN OVERLAYS

Structural design overlays include framing plans, reinforcing layouts, column caps, and schedules. In this phase of the project, the greatest impact of the overlay system may well be the problem-solving aspect during project development. Also there is the potential for improving coordination of such construction activities as layout of foundations and conflicts with utilities.

Production Technique: Architectural Base Sheet Development of structural drawings involves the preparation of floor-framing systems. Unlike other engineering disciplines, structural purposes are not always best served by the architectural floor plan as a base sheet unless, that is, it contains layouts of columns, grids, exterior walls, and interior partitions identified as load-bearing or non-load-bearing. Also needed will be data to indicate special loaded areas where structures may need additional strength (Figure 13-1).

Both architectural and structural development procedures begin with preparation of the basic column framing grid, which is put together by the architect and the engineer (Figure 13-2). Typically, the grid will outline the perimeter of the structure for one particular floor level, usually the ground floor. The complete grid preparation procedure, including the scribe coat process, is described in Chapter 10.

After the template sheet has been prepared and approved, reproducibles are contact-printed for the architect and the structural engineer. Copies of the grid sheet to be used by the architect for the development of floor plan base sheets for the various floors of a project will be photoreproductions on prepunched polyester film with a draftable matte surface one side, and a moist-erasable image.

At this stage decisions about copies for structural use must be made. Are structural overlays to be prepared on blank sheets or on copies of grid sheets? If the grid sheet is to be the base sheet, copying on diazo-sensitized polyester film without a matte surface and with fixed line image is the proper choice. If structural framing plans are to be prepared on the grid sheet, prepunched photoreproducibles with a moist-erasable image and no matte surface are preferable. A number of copies of the framing grid will be needed if the

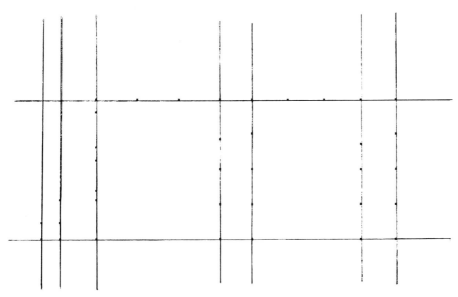

FIGURE 13-1 Framing grid. This overlay is a simple version of a framing grid to be combined with other bases and overlays such as dimensions and column caps.

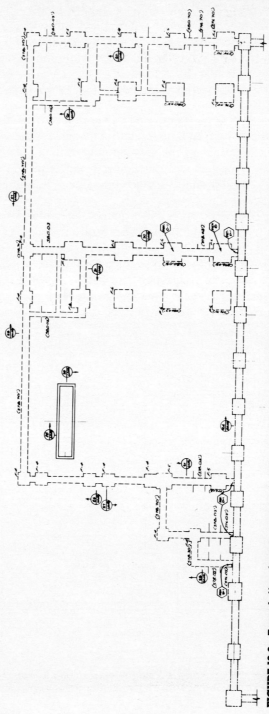

FIGURE 13-2 Foundation framing plan. The final structural drawing is a composite of this base and other overlays such as dimensions, column grid, and schedules. The guiding principle for separation is to classify data subject to change, so that changing one type of data will not disturb other types not needing change. Base sheets prepared separately and available for cost-estimating purposes help make it easier to identify elements for sizing and pricing. (Jewell, Downing & Associates, Architects)

structure being designed is a multilevel project: one for each level for development to completion as a framing plan.

Structural Design Overlays   Overlays are needed for dimensions, steel reinforcement, notes, column caps, and schedules.

Dimension overlay   Use of an overlay to simplify complex data, which dimensions often are, is one way to prevent a careless approach to layout dimensioning by drafting personnel. Proper control to reduce or eliminate repetitive and unnecessary dimensions contributes to the production of clear, accurate drawings and has a beneficial effect on project accomplishments.

The use, for each plan, of one or more dimension overlays, at least one of which is in common with both architectural and structural layouts, helps ease the concerns of coordination and the problems of drawing completion as the project nears schedule deadlines. Since erasing and changing drawings is a critical fraction of the production effort, updating a self-contained overlay for just dimensions is much simpler than attempting to update layouts in a conventionally prepared drawing. Such a drawing is complex, and many items of information are likely to be disturbed by just one simple dimension change.

Another advantage of overlays is to be realized in making changes from English to metric measuring units. Placing the two sets of measurements on separate overlays can minimize the problems of conversion. The problem arises in connection with foreign projects designed locally in areas in which English units are used.

An alternative to this technique is to use an overlay with dimensions in metric; the English units are drawn directly on the base plan. When metric dimensions are needed, the overlay with metric units is printed full strength and the base sheet, with its English measurement units is printed screened, say 50 percent of line strength. The metric units will then stand out clearly and the English units will be subdued.

Steel reinforcing overlay   Placing the layout of steel reinforcing for concrete construction on an overlay offers two important advantages: multicolor printing and construction coordination. Reinforcing layouts will be useful for levels that are similar but have variations in plan that affect slab and beam reinforcing. Separate overlays may then be needed.

The complete framing plan of each floor level is then obtained by compositing base sheets and overlays to achieve efficient production at less cost and with improved clarity. One example is a typical framing grid printed in full line strength with an overlay screened to show a different floor level variation together with another overlay, also screened, to show differences in steel reinforcing. The alternative, for clearer reading drawings, would be offset printing in multicolor.

Notes overlay   The use of overlays for structural purposes is more selective than for other engineering fields, and it should be assessed for production improvement, clarity, and cost savings. An overlay just for notations should have some justification such as to further an early planning decision to use multicolor offset printing. Overlays for schedules are easier to justify; they can be worked on without disturbing the production effort during the preparation of framing plans, for example. The principle that guides overlay use is simplification: If an overlay can solve problems involving data arrangement for notes, details, schedules, and layout information, then the technique should be considered.

Column caps overlay The column caps overlay should be considered for its problem-solving potential, since column caps may affect the installation of various mechanical systems. Whenever structural design includes column caps and there is a chance that conflicts with other trades might occur, or column caps are not to be penetrated by pipes, ducts, or conduit, it is more efficient to have information about the caps furnished to each engineer rather than have each seek the information individually.

PLUMBING AND PIPING SYSTEMS

Every project has some need for simplification of production effort, and that applies to plumbing and piping systems. Such systems usually present difficult layout and planning problems; examples are horizontal and vertical space conflicts, expansion, drainage slope, valving, and insulation. Also, plumbing and piping systems have the broadest range of design elements. One reference source lists over seventy different plumbing and piping systems for which the mechanical engineer has responsibility for meeting health and safety requirements.

Traditionally, the responsibility for the design and installation of plumbing and piping systems has been divided. Plumbing has come under the jurisdiction of the plumbing engineer and piping for mechanical systems has been designed by the mechanical engineer. Yet the two systems have basic theory, materials, and installation in common, so there are practical reasons for combining them on the same drawing or on a related series of overlays. That is particularly true when the mechanical subcontractor is responsible for the installation of the systems regardless of whose drawings they may be located on.

Placing plumbing and piping layouts on either the same overlay or on related overlays logically leads to clearer, easier-to-understand drawings that are successful solutions to the problems of piping congestion, duplications, and omissions. Also, the practice encourages standardization of symbols for interpreting piping and plumbing systems in both black-and-white and color printing.

Decisions about the selection and use of overlays for plumbing and piping systems are influenced both by factors described in the preceding paragraphs and by the specific problem-solving features of the overlay system. For solving the extraordinarily complex layout problems of projects such as power generation stations, mechanical equipment rooms, refineries, and ships, overlay drafting will contrast sharply with such techniques as isometrics and perhaps piping models. In favor of the overlay technique is the potential for structuring intricate systems and designs by levels and by different systems, all at proper scale and in proper relation from system to system horizontally as well as vertically.

Preplanning drawing development is the basis for decisions on the number of plumbing and piping overlay sheets to be prepared to achieve the best possible quality and clarity of details, as well as whiteprinting or offset printing in black and white or multicolor. There is a need for standards setting the colors of different systems to help facilitate both estimating and the actual construction and installation of the systems.

Plumbing and Piping Overlays For some projects the engineer, as an alternative to the conventional grouping of systems on drawings, might consider mechanical, domestic, and special systems in slab layouts and also in ceiling layouts.

Coordination Technique An engineer's reaction to the overlay system, despite its clearly apparent economic benefits, can too easily be negative if the architect, as the leader, falls short of making a proper contribution during the documentation. Two areas in particular require constant attention:

Quality of architectural documentation Basic and supplemental information, base sheets, and clarification printing must be accurate and legible to spare the engineer from redoing work because inadequate data have been furnished by the architect.

When changes in architectural data occur, all team members must be notified promptly and consistently by methods and materials that can make the updating of drawings easy. In form, the notification might be marked-up whiteprints, freehand sketches, or perhaps just memos—whatever will make the changes easy to make accurately and simply.

Again, engineers and consultants never make changes on base sheets, the background data used for development of overlays. They make changes only in their own work. They are entitled to architect responsiveness to their needs and architect initiative in keeping everyone up to date on changes so that progress is maintained and no team member incurs unnecessary expenses or suffers production delays. The greater the initiative the architect takes in communicating with engineers and consultants, the more effective coordination will be.

Currency of information The standard procedure is to distribute vital project data as soon as it is confirmed. Unfortunately, the odious principle of "right to know" that guides some professionals prevents the needed data from reaching those who are in need of it. Not every professional will know exactly who should be provided with what, so it is in the best interests of the project to give information wide distribution. One way to do so is to establish a distribution list early in the project-planning stage.

Composites Normally, the architect arranges for the reproduction of base sheets and overlays assembled into final drawings, the layered composites.

These will be based on the previously established drawing index. Sometimes the engineer is in a better position to get composites made and may be asked to arrange for the printing from the architect's base sheet and the engineer's overlay sheet or sheets. Such a print might be produced in-house, if the capability is there, or by a reprographics firm.

Before final printing is ordered, and during the course of the work, the architect and engineer may wish to review the finished base sheet and overlays—both architectural and engineering—to determine the value of composites other than the usual final project drawings. For example, a structural framing plan might be combined with a layout for pipes embedded in slabs, rather than hung in ceiling plenums, in order to spot expensive conflicts.

HEATING, VENTILATING, AND AIR-CONDITIONING

Heating, ventilating, and air-conditioning systems that warrant use of overlays include fresh air supply ductwork, exhaust air ductwork, return air, contaminated air, and fire-protected exhaust ductwork. A principal overlay goal is efficiently and clearly shown construction data that sometimes may be little more than diagrammatic. Like any other building element, ductwork systems occupy space—sometimes more space than is realized by installation crews. Therefore, their positions within the structure require accurate layout data that reflects sizes of material and equipment to be installed and the space available for the installation.

Base Sheet Production Depending on the type of project being designed, the engineer may need base sheet data from two sources: the architect and the structural engineer. One base sheet will show spaces, and the other will show structural elements that may influence placement of equipment and material. The data can be combined by the versatile overlay system to facilitate system design and layout. The combined base sheet might, for example, consist of the architectural floor plan and a structural framing plan screened or toned down, and it might also show column caps if they are used and are important. It would be a special base sheet for planning purposes only. It would enable the engineer to design and do layout work on an overlay without having to spend much time in searching for data that could affect the layout of ducts and equipment.

The special base sheet also offers the advantage of improved checking and coordination. With it the structural engineer finds it easier to verify that the structure will not be affected by mechanical system penetration of slabs, beams, and column caps and that floor openings and duct passages coincide.

System Efficiency As pointed out in preceding chapters, the mechanical engineer profits from overlay techniques in two fundamental ways:

1. The separation of data or layouts on individual sheets leads to quicker

and more versatile preparation of clear and easy-to-understand products such as multicolor printing.

2. Economic gains are realized by not having to draw floor plans, erase plans, and make corrections.

Related Overlays The mechanical engineer's design is normally done in conjunction with overlays, prepared by other team members, for the reflected ceiling plan, lighting and communication, and the sprinkler system (Figure 13-3). Such data might not otherwise be available to the mechanical engineer. Team members should be kept informed of data being created and developed and be provided with copies of it as soon as possible.

ELECTRICAL DESIGN

It is not always apparent how dependent electrical design is on the early receipt of reference data from all team members, particularly since it tends to be one of the last elements of a project to be completed. Furnishing data promptly and stressing the coordination of electrical engineers and other team members is one way to shorten the time of project development. All engineers and their staffs need to become well acquainted with and proficient in the overlay system fundamentals described in Chapters 6 and 7: registration bars, prepunched polyester drafting film, the reference and background data on base sheets, and production techniques.

Base Sheet Production

Plans The typical base sheet used by the electrical engineer for development of layouts for lighting, power circuiting, communications, and alarm systems is the architectural floor plan. The engineer usually receives a copy made on diazo-sensitized polyester film punched for registration.

Building sections The electrical engineer will also benefit from a base sheet developed by the architect to show interior elevations of mechanical equipment areas and profiles of building sections, both cross-sectional and longitudinal. These drawing features can be used to show vertical risers, panels, and junction boxes.

Supplemental Overlays Primary information that relates to electrical systems includes schedules of equipment, together with power requirements, and coordinated layouts that accurately locate and size all equipment and devices that use electricity. Overlays help the engineer eliminate repetitive drafting and reduce errors and omissions.

Electrical layouts also show the locations and sizes of the electrical equipment required by other disciplines such as pumps, duct heaters, motors, elevators, power doors, and power equipment. If the detail provided by the architect can be used by those responsible for such project features, then the work of each of the other team members can be shown on overlays for eventual composition with the architectural background base sheet of sec-

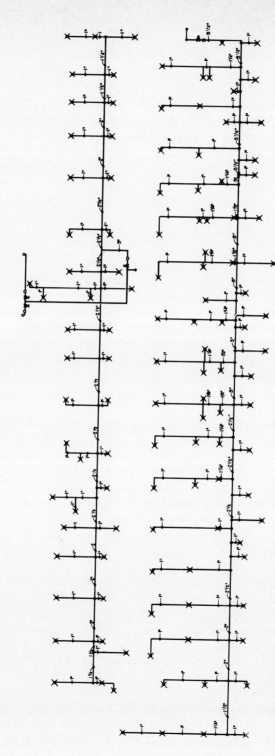

FIGURE 13-3 Sprinkler plan overlay. (Jewell, Downing & Associates, Architects)

tions. The usual tendency in project development is to have the electrical engineer search all drawings for such project features whenever progress prints are distributed to the members of the project. The skillful coordination of this production responsibility can have profound influence on progress and the meeting of deadlines.

Lighting Overlays Lighting overlays, while simplifying professional effort, help reduce the time lag that often occurs between the development of electrical drawings and the work of other disciplines (Figure 13-4). The ideal is to have all work completed at about the same time without undue pressure upon any single discipline.

The overlay process begins with the architect providing the engineer with a diazo reproduction of the base sheet, usually a floor plan, punched for registration. It may also be a composite of the floor plan with the ceiling plan produced by the diazo process on polyester film. The engineer places this sheet on the drafting board and pins it to the registry bar at the top of the sheet. A new sheet for drafting purposes is placed over the base sheet and it too is pinned to the registration bar. The overlay sheet, the typical system unit, is a punched sheet of 4-mil polyester film with a draftable matte surface on one side.

After the lighting plan is approved, the engineer has the option of placing the circuiting and switching directly on the overlay or on a separate overlay. The final, formal drawing for construction is a composite of the base sheet, lighting plan, and ceiling plan.

Electrical Riser Layout The overlay for the electrical riser layout is prepared over a building section. Its primary value is in coordination during construction.

Power Overlay A separate power overlay permits drafting of the electrical power system to proceed in a logical, methodical manner without disrupting the development of other electrical design drawings.

Legends and Symbols Overlays Standard symbols are in general use, but a uniform way to record them has yet to be established. One simple way, made available by the overlay system, could be the following:

1. One composite sheet of symbols is prepared for the standards of all disciplines.

2. The composite can be made up of a series of overlays each of which contains certain categories of information: abbreviations, general notes, drafting symbols, material indications, and plumbing, mechanical, and electrical symbols.

3. Each category can be drawn in a planned position on its own overlay sheet so it can be composited with the standards sheet or with a floor plan, system overlay, or symbol overlay.

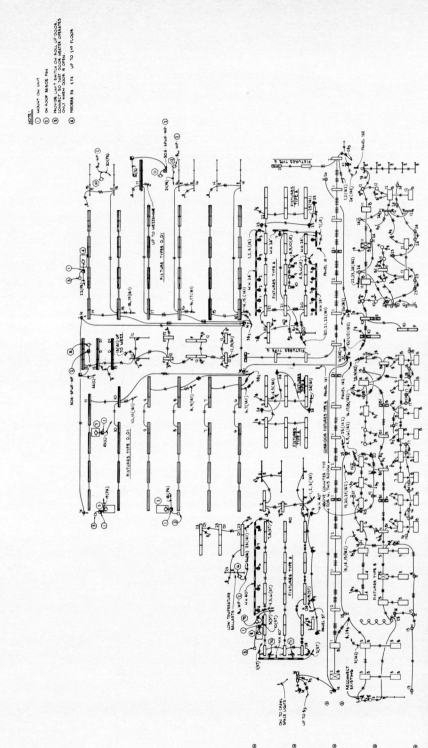

FIGURE 13-4 Lighting plan overlay. (Jewell, Downing & Associates, Architects)

CHAPTER FOURTEEN

Construction Mode Drawings

What is so exceptional about the overlay technique that makes it desirable as the production standard for the professional office?

One question leads to another. Everything new offered to the architect as a better way invariably raises the question, "What's in it for me?" And there are important answers. One is that, with a successful overlay production background, the architect has little trouble in dealing with clients and builders who also feel the right to ask, of this versatile new development, "What's in it for me?"

There are specific benefits for the builder, the client, and concerned government agencies, as well as the architect. Those for the builder include:

- Improvements in quantity takeoff and cost estimates
- Coordination of design during layout of foundation and various floor levels
- Shop drawing development
- Visual aids for meetings

Those for the client include:

- As-built record drawings
- Presentations for meetings
- Reduced job extras
- Recurring layout changes and lease allocations

Benefits for government agencies include a clearer definition of hazardous, security, assembly, and contaminated areas and of fire and health protection, walls, partitions, and areas.

The architect gets unique and attractive covers for drawings and specifications, brochures, and design competitions and has an easier start on subsequent related projects.

All those benefits, all those improvements in professional services, are available through skilled utilization of the overlay technique. They are discussed in the balance of this chapter.

BUILDER BENEFITS

The financial aspects of construction involve feasibility surveys, budget development, quantity surveys, estimates, and contract negotiations. During the bidding process, overlays printed separately from base sheets clearly identify specialties to be priced. Size, type, quantity, and use of material and equipment to be furnished and installed must be specified. The overlay for any particular element of work to be priced is the pricing format. It shows only the work of a particular subcontractor or contractor. For estimating purposes, it is a relatively simple instrument free of clutter in comparison with a drawing usually available for cost estimating (Figure 13-2).

Prepared by the engineer, the overlay shows only related data, and nothing on the drawing confuses the estimator or the installer. The use of individual overlay sheets for estimating purposes is a specialized feature of construction documents; and since there is no established practice, the architect may list overlays separately from conventional drawings as supplemental data available at extra cost. Certainly the pricing of work from overlay sheets helps the estimator be accurate.

Construction Drawings Construction drawings produced in the conventional way are essentially a matter of convenience to the preparer, whether architect or engineer. Up to now it has not been practical or economical to produce them in ways that conform to actual construction processes. And until now there has been little reason to expect changes for the better. The overlay technique can exert a considerable influence on traditions, particularly for the management of fast-track and phased construction, the newer developments in the construction field. Since the primary purpose of a construction drawing is to convey data regarding methods, materials, sizes, quantities, and responsibilities, the information on drawings is more useful if it is assembled and portrayed to show more direct relations of procedures, material, and related construction activities. Overlays make that assembly and portrayal possible.

Site Layout Planning Just as the owner of a building needs a plan for space uses, so the builder needs a plan for laying out construction processes, the counterpart of a factory production line to guide work activities. This includes the entire range of site activities: the placement of construction trailers and offices, storage points for materials and equipment, access to the site, fences and their design, and restricted areas.

Underground Utilities In projects with extensive underground utility work overlays will be found useful for coordinating and scheduling trenching and the installation of pipe and structures. The first step is to determine which overlay system drawings can be used. Information that might be needed includes:

1. Property lines and profiles of buildings, structures, and paving, data that usually appears on base sheets.

2. Utilities: sewer, water, storm drainage, electricity, gas, and telephone.

That information can be compiled by different disciplines on different drawings or overlays. To achieve a coordinated drawing, the overlay sheets bearing the data needed are combined to produce a composite that shows both site conditions and utilities. Such a composite can be obtained from a reproduction facility through the architect at the contractor's cost.

The format of the composite will normally differ from that used by the architect, particularly if the drawing is to contain references to the builder and coordination data not normally a part of the architect's design responsibilities. The question of legal responsibilities arises when the architect's drawings are used in this manner and additional data is placed on them by people not within the architect's jurisdiction.

If a composite is produced and the contractor plans to add coordination data for use by subcontractors, a drawing similar to a shop drawing might be made by either diazo or photoreproduction. The architect could advise the contractor on the method preferred. A composite produced to help the contractor cope with coordination might have the following data added by the contractor's own forces:

1. Borders and title block with a drawing title such as Utility-Trenching Layout Drawing.

2. Benchmarks, monuments, and elevations (inverts) of pipe and conduit.

3. Trench layouts showing limits of excavation—width, depth, and length—by using dashed lines.

4. Phasing data illustrating the sequence of trenching construction and backfilling: starting points, direction of excavation, starting time, completion phases, and backfill. The drawing might also contain details and other data for shoring that might be required by legal authorities to ensure safety during construction.

5. Scheduling data related to sequence and priority both of site work and of connections and extensions within the structure.

The coordination process continues with the issuing of prints of the special drawing to subcontractors and material suppliers for feedback on deliveries and construction work. Early involvement of subcontractors and material suppliers should cut down on conflicts and misunderstandings and the redoing of site work. Again, the major objectives of this management tool are to approach and resolve problems at the planning stage and to limit errors and omissions to the drafting board. Picturization of trenching, utilities, and structures to be built on the site will help simplify the problems of the most complex site project.

Layout of Foundation and Floor Levels   The overlay system opens the way to important new interpretations of construction drawings. By using overlays, drawings can be produced in various formats that are quite different from those of conventional drawings. Information can be logically related to the actual building process. In conventional drawings, information is separated by disciplines and the contractor has to refer to a series of individual sheets to locate and relate data. To achieve coordination, the only option available is to transfer information from one drawing to another, often by using colored crayon for marking prints.

By using overlay system drawings, the potential for errors and misunderstandings can be either eliminated or substantially reduced. The method described here involves compositing a certain group of drawing sheets to assemble construction data in a nonconventional format, construction mode drawing. As one example of this different approach, a number of architect- and engineer-produced base sheets and overlays are printed as a composite:

1. Floor plan screened 50 percent
2. Structural framing plan in full line strength
3. Reinforcing layout printed in color
4. Pipes and conduit embedded in concrete slabs printed in color
5. Pipes and conduit below floor slabs printed in color
6. Risers—piping, conduit, and ductwork—printed in color

By this method, problems of coordination are simplified and confined to a print. Conflicts, errors, and omissions are easier to detect, and risers through slabs that miss formed openings or dimensioned sleeves are visible, detectable, and correctable before any expensive rework is required.

Some cautions must be observed. The contractor must be made aware of the potential of the overlay approach and must be guided by the architect to gain from the technique. Also, multicolor printing in small quantities is expensive. For that reason the technique must be given early consideration. Printing in color after bidding, just for the low bidder's use during construction, is also practical. The expense must, however, be borne by the contractor.

Shop Drawings   A critical need of the entire construction process is a way to shorten the turnaround time for preparation, submittal, and review of shop drawings. In conventional drawing production, shop drawings are prepared by suppliers and subcontractors as original drawings. Usually they resemble the drawings prepared by the design professionals; often they duplicate data on the drawings prepared for bidding. A system that would eliminate duplication of effort and reduce the intricate review procedure that consumes excessive time and expense has long been needed. A logical move in that direction is to reuse the architect's and engineer's drawings by making reproducible copies of them for subcontractor use. The following is a typical shop drawing development procedure:

From the architect the contractor obtains a reproducible copy made by either the diazo or the photo process. An example might be a ceiling plan with a lighting layout. Involved in the work required for that feature of the building would be ceiling installation, lighting, sheet metal, piping, and access panels. Each subcontractor would be required to indicate corrections and changes in layout on a separate print. The changes and corrections would be transferred by hand to the reproducible.

An alternative procedure would be to make the changes on reproducible copies of separate overlays for the various trades. From those overlays and a base sheet a composite would be made to show the coordinated efforts of the subcontractors. The coordinated composite, the product of the shop drawing process, would then be submitted for the architect's review rather than a stack of whiteprints, many of which are often thrown away during the review process. Occasionally, a copy of the contractor's transmittal form is all that is needed by some parties to the administration of the project.

The single reproducible submitted by the contractor for some particular phase or area of work will be subject to further changes by either the architect or the engineer or both. In its final, approved form it may eventually be submitted to the building owner for as-built documentation. The title block data will relate to the general contractor, and not to the architect or engineer.

When shop drawings must be submitted long distances, savings in mailing costs can be achieved by converting the full-size reproducibles to either photographic reduction negatives made on the process camera-projector unit or microfilms. The negatives or microfilms are transmitted to the supplier, who then makes prints for review locally, marks them with changes and corrections, and returns them to the general contractor for approval. The alternative is to go through the hand-drafting routine of changes and corrections on a full-size diazo or photoreproduction that is then converted back to either a reduction negative or microfilm and returned to the contractor and architect for approval.

Visual Aids for Meetings Productive coordination occurs when key team members meet and contribute their special expertise to solutions of the entire range of construction problems. Prints are the common form of coordination data, but their use during large conferences has serious drawbacks. The most serious drawback is the distraction caused by the large numbers of sheets of drawings needed for such meetings.

The overlay system makes it possible to employ a simpler visual aid conference technique. Two visual aids that can improve coordination meeting productivity are microfilm and the positive transparencies usually referred to as Vu-Graphs (Figure 14-1). Registered microfilm is not yet possible, but it is possible and feasible to employ registered transparencies.

Positive transparencies are made directly from the reduction negatives of architects' and engineers' drawings. The usual size is 8½ by 11 in punched for mounting on a three-pin registration bar, which can be placed directly on the top of the overhead projection unit for projection onto either a large screen or a portable screen. The registration of positive transparencies, which are usually made of acetate, will match exactly that of the reduction negative and the original tracings. Positive transparencies are available in a range of colors, and that makes it possible for individual overlays to be projected in color onto a screen. During projection, the individual base and overlay transparencies can be superimposed on one another and pinned together on the three-pin registry bar. They are then projected together on the screen for examination of construction features and systems. Team members can thereby get a clear

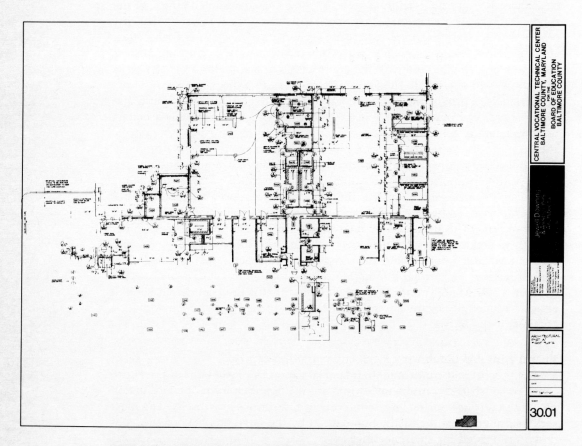

FIGURE 14-1 Vu-Graph of a composite of Figures 7-1, 10-4, and 10-6. It shows the technique for building up composites in a wide variety to suit any special project requirement. Here the need is to inform a number of people simultaneously. (Jewell, Downing and Associates, Architects, Baltimore, Md.)

understanding of the nature of the project. The following is an example of how positive transparencies can be used with an overhead projector for coordination purposes:

- The structural framing plan is pinned to the bar first. It can be produced in color or just black line.
- Over it is pinned the plumbing or piping overlay produced in a different color.

When those two drawings are displayed on the screen, the various subcontractors for concrete, plumbing, mechanical, and electrical work can discuss conflicts, omissions, drawing errors, and schedules. Also discussed might be materials that must be placed within concrete forms, locations of pipe sleeves, duct openings in slabs, priorities of forming for special-equipment installations, platforms, sloping slabs, differing slab levels, and curbs.

The advantage of this coordination technique is the improved ability to control meetings by concentrating attention of all those present on just the graphic data on display. In the course of the meeting, the participants either mark up their own copies of drawings for their particular work or make notes for later transfer to their copies of drawings.

BENEFITS FOR THE CLIENT

As-Built Record Drawings   There is no disagreement that the architect and the contractor have a common interest in getting the highest quality of design and detail in the completed structure. Yet within the industry there is a real need to prescribe standards of quality of the construction records to be delivered to the client. Because of the lack of any agreed-upon standards, the responsibility for complete, accurate records is usually unspecified even when there is a contract agreement for their delivery to the owner upon completion of all work. Two facts should be apparent:

1. Accurate records are important to the project owner.
2. The responsibility for proper record accumulation and preparation should be accepted by all those who provide the records.

Actually, high-quality records are a relatively minor matter in the administration of a project, and an objective of the overlay system is to provide ways to simplify their preparation and to encourage more interest in the subject. When it is derived through overlay techniques, construction documentation can be produced with the same quality as documentation produced by the design professional.

The methods available to the contractor and the subcontractors depend on the use of either diazo or photoreproduction copies of the base sheet and overlays produced by the design team. These copies may be limited to floor plan base sheets, system layouts, and special space layouts on overlays, all reproduced on moist-erasable polyester film prepunched for registration. At the conclusion of the construction work, the updated reproducibles are delivered to the owner together with shop drawings, catalog cuts, and operating manuals, all properly classified and indexed.

Presentations for Meetings   The client, as a project owner, can benefit from the overlay system by using multicolor printing, pin-registered superimposition of base sheet and overlays, or overhead projection of positive transparencies for making presentations at meetings. Visual aids are discussed later in this chapter.

Reduced Job Extras   When the project budget includes a contingency factor to cover the cost of "unanticipated" job extras, the project owner has few friends and weapons to help safeguard the fund and many enemies with many weapons wanting to appropriate it. The contingency fund, often a considerable amount of money, is a prime target of the entire building team. A sizable amount of manpower and legal and technical expertise is concentrated on discovering weaknesses in the contract documents that can be exploited at the expense of the fund. The project owner is usually badly outnumbered.

The contingency fund may even appeal to the architect who is compensated by a fee related to the total project cost. The architect's responsibility regarding the contingency fund is usually vague, yet the project owner has few other means of protecting the fund from erosion by job extras for changed work and errors and omissions in the contract documents: the project drawings and specifications.

As a rule, the project owner has few options but to write off the contingency fund at the beginning of construction unless the architect has demonstrated competence and construction know-how or there is a way to produce drawings of better quality and coordination capability to keep job changes and extras under control. The quality of drawings is often reflected in the number and amount of job extras; the quality of construction begins with the quality of drawings and production technology possessed by the architect. And that is all the project owner can rely on. When construction gets underway and job extras begin to appear, it is too late to judge the quality of drawings. The overlay system has the potential of providing the project owner with some degree of protection for the contingency fund when the architect takes the initiative to employ it—and, incidentally, demonstrate technical competence.

Recurring Layout Changes; Lease Allocations   Some projects will require additional drawings to be made after all construction work is complete. These will be for office and space assignments, space leasing, furniture and fixture layouts. All are subject to change from time to time. Space modifications and alterations often involve changes in plumbing and electrical ductwork that can be accommodated much easier by using copies of the architect's and engineer's base sheets and overlays. Such copies would be either diazo or photoreproductions on punched sheets of polyester film with a moist-erasable image. If the project owner were to use the pin register technique with base sheet and overlays for layout and system changes within a building, the architect's guidance would be required.

BENEFITS FOR GOVERNMENT AND REGULATORY AGENCIES

It is usually a chore for the professional plan reviewer in the building permit office to analyze the health and safety measures designed into a project for compliance with code requirements. Few efforts are made by architects to isolate and identify special building areas and legal requirements for occupancy, numbers, size and locations of exits, routes and means of egress, special considerations for hazardous, contaminated areas, fire protection, qualities of basic construction and finish materials, and continuity of protection.

Usually from the architect's point of view it is the plan reviewer's responsibility to make code compliance determinations. Most architects have a general awareness of just what will comply with the code, even though few large projects make it through a permit review without suffering many changes.

The established procedure for review and determination of compliance with code requirements has two weaknesses: usually more time is needed to review and process a project than should be needed, and changes in drawings are more expensive than they should be. The entire process can be simplified and shortened by using the overlay technique in conjunction with appliqué sheet drafting materials and press-on pattern tapes. Here are some suggestions:

1. Tapes to indicate the thickness, material, and fire protection rating of walls and partitions and the continuity of protection from slab to slab and from slab to ceiling.

2. Shading films to show exit corridors, direction of travel, and the location and size of exits.

3. Other shading films to identify the space and occupancy limits.

4. A mechanical system overlay to show hazardous and contaminated areas and the means of control and disposition of the exhausted air.

The overlay method has the added advantage of making it easier to interpret the often complex and confusing code terminology and relate it to specific job conditions.

ARCHITECT BENEFITS

When does an architect's exposure to publicity begin? A brochure may be the start, but exposure and promotion are synonymous. The architect promotes for business development, but the first broad exposure to those in the construction process is with the construction documents. For that exposure, the covers of drawings and specifications are as important to the architect as the covers of any high-fashion magazine are to the publisher (Figure 10-2). No publisher of a high-quality magazine could possibly be satisfied with quality that satisfies many architect-publishers. A client may be impressed with the talent of the architect as exhibited in a brochure and be distressed by the quality of construction documents. Any architect who wants to exploit all promotion possibilities must seriously consider project cover sheets.

Brochures   It is a simple step from expertly designed covers of project construction documents to office promotion brochures. The overlay technique is used in conjunction with photodrafting, scissors drafting, and cut and paste.

Design Competitions   One challenge that appeals to architects but not all accept is the occasional design competition. Why do such architectural events not attract more architects? Not enough time? Too busy? Too much work? Too expensive? Lack of confidence? After all, the true appeal of the design competition to the ambitious architect is the chance to display talent and be original and creative, which is not always possible with every client commission. With all the production technology available for simple, quick solutions to drawing preparation, which makes more time available for design efforts, competitions should have a built-in appeal for architects who are knowledgeable and experienced in reprographic techniques and the overlay system.

Easier Start on Subsequent Projects   One factor that should appeal to both the building owner and the architect is the opportunity to get addition and alteration projects designed quicker and at lower cost if the original project has been designed with up-to-date production technology. The owner profits, and the architect is in a position to handle more business—repeat business—with a better chance to improve profitability. The opportunity to produce addition and alteration work in a shorter time and at lower cost should be an important factor in an architect's decision to adopt the overlay system.

Visual Aids   To sell a project to a client is not the easiest professional task. Often there is the matter of communication. The architect has one perspective and speaks one language, and the client and the client's staff, board of directors, and committee are not acquainted with important construction terminology. An audiovisual presentation based on 35-mm slides or positive transparencies breaks down the language barrier, particularly since it focuses everyone's attention on the architect's presentation.

A presentation has two important objectives: to make the project understandable in all respects and to make certain that the project accurately defines the client's building needs and the architect has not added any features not requested by the client. Again, an architect who is fully acquainted with production technology and with reprographic capability finds the task of preparing an important presentation not nearly as expensive or time-consuming as by the conventional method of using only a large number of full-size drawings.

Professionalism with limits   Where does professionalism in architecture stop? Certainly few architects can afford to stop at design. Today, there is more to it than that. Practical matters such as making a profit to stay in business demand that the architect have expertise in all aspects of practice. The modern architect must be fluent in more than the language of design aesthetics; production and management technology have other languages to be mastered. As the use of advanced technology becomes more prevalent, an architect who can speak eloquently about it has an answer for the client, contractor, or government official who asks, "This new idea, overlay drafting, what's in it for me?"

CHAPTER FIFTEEN

Overlays and Computer-Aided Design

A revolution in drafting room practice took place in the 1960s, and by now, it would be expected, the entire architectural profession should have profited from the experience and teaching of pioneers. All offices, large and small, should be making use of modern practices that are standard in leading firms. But it is quite clear that a very large percentage of offices do not regard production know-how as a technology they must master to remain competitive in services and quality of practice. The reason might be that architectural executives are not open-minded, or it may be that educators are slow to realize the influence of drafting room success on practice success. Whatever the reason, today anyone can understand the need for technical superiority in the drafting room and learn how to get it. Learning how to identify an effective capability is probably the most formidable obstacle for some architects to overcome. They have to contend with heavy promotion of wide-ranging drafting shortcuts and the newest: computer-aided design (CAD).

Although the future of drafting room productivity may be difficult for some to comprehend, it is clearly centered around the entirely new standard called pin graphics. A practical approach to methodology, pin graphics offers all the known strengths of drafting productivity including the newest, computer-aided drafting and design (CADD). Included in the new standard are the overlay technique, systems drafting, reprographics, graphic arts, and sophisticated industrial reprography, as well as CAD.

Of all drafting room techniques, the one that has excited interest in greater productivity is CAD. Its promoters are likely to take exception to classifying

CAD as merely a component of pin graphics, but as the experience of users of CAD continues to be recorded, it becomes quite clear that those who are gaining the most from CAD use have to rely on the best of other reprographic techniques. Also, it is becoming an accepted fact that the combination of CAD and overlay has evolved as the best foundation for effective production that is available to the design professional. And because the cost of computers continues to drop dramatically, it is apparent there will be an explosive growth in computer use. All architects should prepare for the computer age by learning all they can about both CAD and the overlay system. There is a solid relation between the two that has been eloquently pictured by the architect who termed CAD "the electronic pin bar."

To better understand the overlay-based potential of CAD, architects must know about the reactions of successful computer users that shed some light on the value of CAD. One of them says, "The process of selecting and acquiring the right CAD system is complex and has implications far beyond cost." Another states, "CAD doesn't automatically increase productivity and lower costs, the main benefit is quality." From those statements it can be seen that knowing what CAD can and can not do is not easy to establish, and the task of finding out is much more difficult if the factor of management is overlooked.

There is no shortage of claims about computer advantages, but there is a decided shortage of publicity about computer shortcomings. In the following section, which emphasizes the relations of CAD and the overlay system, the limitations of CAD are evident and so are the invaluable advantages and benefits.

CAD and Productivity   To begin with, certain decisions are made in regard to both hardware and software designed for architectural procedures. They are made with qualified assistance, so they will not be considered here. Our first question is just what should the architect want the computer to do. The following is a fairly complete list.

Design	Sales
Working drawings	Government agencies
Plans	Manpower planning
Elevations	Interviews
Sections	Equipment schedules
Details	Finish schedules
Computations	Furnishings
Scheduling	Legends
Payroll	Keynotes
Finances	Symbols
Marketing	Abbreviations
Summary and status reports	

Computer companies have an optimistic view of CAD's potential for architectural use; claims range from a ratio of 1 to 1 to as much as 100 to 1. There is general agreement that CAD can be responsible for as much as 35 percent of the total drawing package, whereas some of the most enthusiastic CAD believers are looking for 100 percent computer use. Consider first the high and low claims of 100 to 1 and 1 to 1. What are they in reference to?

The 100 to 1 advantage usually applies to repetitive drafting chores such as detailing material indications, the sort of task most architects would like to be freed from. On the other hand, the 1 to 1 ratio usually applies to more complex tasks such as the preparation of floor plans. It may come as a shock to architects who are seriously considering a CAD investment to learn that it normally takes as much time to produce a floor plan on the computer as it does to produce it by the overlay technique. Note that the comparison is with production by overlay, and not by traditional methods. Overlay has the advantage in this respect.

At this point we should give some attention to the efficiency factor, which influences all architectural production effort and therefore applies to both CAD and overlay systems. It is one thing to make a substantial investment in CAD or adopt the overlay technique for the drafting room, but it is another to get the most out of either. The one glaring weakness in production is a lack of attention to efficiency. Few if any architects go so far as to conduct time-and-motion studies on any drafting procedure, but there are plenty of unsound generalizations about the savings in time and cost to be achieved through such shortcuts as scissors drafting and paste-up. The claims, ranging from 5 to 95 percent savings, are based mainly on hope that expectations have been met. Unfortunately, few architects have the time or inclination to devise scientific proof of efficiency in production. Perhaps it really is not necessary, but it is a factor that should not be overlooked in any phase of the production process, and it is particularly important in the application of both overlay systems and CAD.

There are no performance standards to use as a guide for decisions about selection of any type of production method even though efficient techniques have been taught for a long time. The most elementary example is the production of a floor plan. Often this is the most puzzling of all production tasks, yet it is one that offers measurable elements of a performance standard. A floor plan is developed through orderly systematic processes that are easily defined for the control of drafting personnel, whose attention may be diverted to tasks other than production. The floor plan development technique is to build a plan in the same way that construction will proceed: Start with a grid and then proceed to columns, exterior walls, windows, and key interior features such as elevator shafts, stairs, and interior partitions.

Sources of the data needed to produce a floor plan include the client, consultants, other architects, engineers, government agencies, and contractors. Information is funneled by all sources to the architect, who selects and arranges data in an orderly manner so priorities can be determined. The objective is a drawing that grows steadily, efficiently, and with the fewest unnecessary interruptions in progress.

The process should promote progress within both the architectural office and the engineering services. Drawing "growth" demands that the architect put first things first and resist the temptation to develop secondary information, which will be needed eventually but is not necessary during initial development. The development techniques are usually the least understood of all, and they apply to the development of data on the computer as much as they do to hand production on the drafting board.

Next is the practical matter of relating drawing production by computer to the use of the overlay technique. The two production methodologies are similar, and when overlay is appropriate for use, the investment costs are much lower. There are no performance standards to guide an architect in the selection of production method, but the comparisons given here may help make the choices a little clearer.

Production Since some computers, when matched to appropriate software, can produce basic floor plan data, the architect must give some thought to the fatigue factor. Does working with a small green CRT screen cause an excessive amount of fatigue that may influence both production and quality? At the time of writing there were no studies to guide an architect in this potential problem area.

After considering the factors of potential fatigue, computer operating expense, and production time, another problem arises if the architect decides to prepare a floor plan manually by using the overlay technique. If the production sheets are to be punched polyester film and the computer is to be used for producing other project data on overlays, how does the computer output get registered to the floor plan? This is not a simple question, and the architect needs the proper equipment and the know-how to answer it. Help should come from the computer manufacturer.

Both CAD and the overlay system add to management pressures. With CAD, management is always facing the prospect of inefficient use of the computer's speed and versatility. Output must be paced and intermingled with manual labor to avoid unplanned downtime when no input data is ready for the computer. Then too, if the computer is to be used for other in-house purposes such as manpower or financial planning, another management problem can evolve from use conflicts.

Of all the production advantages the architect can gain from the use of CAD, two are in the important areas of detail enlargement and revisions. Some architects who realize that data input for plan production is equal to board output concentrate attention on superb CAD quality but also strive to take advantage of other important gains involving changes to drawings. As one architect puts it, the second time around is free when the computer is used to create the floor plan, even if there is some cost in time. To a certain extent, that is, gain is usually dependent on the nature of the work.

The time span of changes in work is critical. It costs money to operate a computer, and it takes time to feed input and get output on hard copy, which, of course, has to be compatible with other data forms. Management then relates those values to board time and decides which way to go, CAD or hand drafting. The enlargement capabilities of CAD are impressive, but again management should relate the total CAD capability to the combination of hand work and photo reproduction. One of the important strengths of pin graphics is process photography as described in Chapter 6; the camera-projector unit is capable of outstanding versatility and quality and serves to add vital production capability to the entire pin graphics concept. A modern reprographic plant is an essential element of drafting room production and pin graphics.

The Computer Output Source: The Plotter   It is one thing to get data on the CRT of a computer; what becomes of it is another matter. The data inside the computer has little value unless the architect can get it reproduced in some usable form. That is what the plotter does, and yet few architects are fully knowledgeable about this computer output device. The following example illustrates its importance.

At a certain point in project development, a client requests ten sets of project drawings for progress review. The project at this particular point consists of 100 complete drawings (composites) plus individual base and overlay sheets for a total of 300 sheets, all produced as computer output. The project manager makes out a printing order, checks the files, and learns to his dismay that all file drawings are out of date—all the valid data is *inside* the computer. Now the problem is how to get it out. If the plotter can produce pin-registered composites on punched sheets of polyester film the sheets can be sent to the reprographics firm for making the necessary prints.

The first problem is the output speed of the plotter. The output time of some plotters that can produce ink on film can be as much as 1 hr. Now some simple arithmetic tells us that 1 hr times 100 sheets equals 100 hr, and the client wants the prints as soon as possible. That adds up to 4 days the computer must be producing, three shifts a day. Quite a load on the computer. Then consider all the other things that may happen, such as power outages, the computer being needed for other in-house use and the need for changes right in the middle of the computer run. Any reruns on the computer extend the computer output time and erode client confidence in the architect's abilities. Add to that the potential problems of the plotter running out of ink or skipping, which leaves voids in lines. Plotter downtime adds to production time.

However, if this is a pin graphics project, the manager has the opportunity to make changes on base sheets and overlays quickly and without disrupting computer output. Realistically, there is not much chance of it working that way because the amount of project output by computer will normally range from 20 to 60 percent. Those figures will change, however, as computers are improved, and that is one area in which architects must work for continuing advancement.

Next come the specifics of plotter equipment. The so-called hard-copy computer output device was originally mechanically driven; but technological advances have made electronic types possible, so the choice of plotter is no longer easy or inexpensive. The plotter of today can represent as much as 60 percent of the cost of the computer system. Some architects may not realize they actually had a choice in plotter selection, and as a result they could not use the computer for all they had originally intended.

Plotter types   The groups of plotters include pen, electrostatic, photo, and electron beam recording (EBR). *Pen plotters* produce ink output, and the size capability of pen plotters can vary drastically. Some plotters will produce lines; others only letters. Pen, or vector, plotters can be noisy and may require separate quarters; they may involve large, heavy boxes of paper that require abundant storage facilities. They may produce high temperatures, and so they need special wiring, security, and fire protection.

Sheet materials include paper and film. Some plotters produce only on paper that is sprocket-punched, and therefore they cannot produce punched sheets of film pin-registered for base and overlay production. Other plotters have paper-carrying transports and are not sprocket-punched. CAD output plotted on paper may have a number of disadvantages:

1. Accuracy may be offset when the paper is not dimensionally stable.

2. Images plotted on film may be distorted if produced on a rotary rather than a flatbed plotter.

3. Some manufacturers make sheet products that fit only their plotters.

4. Paper with the wrong rag content can result in clogged, worn pens.

Electrostatic plotters are faster than pen plotters, but they are as much as twice the cost of pen plotters and are not compatible with all computers available to the architect. There is a real possibility that a computer system can quickly become obsolete as computers are improved.

Electronic plotters are capable of superb quality on film as negatives. Once again, management of such plotters can become a real problem if, for instance, output is on a reduction negative and full-size originals must be produced on punched film for, say, progress printing. Such expenses need to be related to speed, accuracy, and quality of production.

Involvement with Pin Graphics   The future of drafting departments is tied to involvement with *pin graphics.* Traditional methods are obsolete, although drawing proficiency will always be an elementary requirement of architectural skills. Drafting room production is now a complex technology involving the essential elements of management, computers, and overlay production techniques, and it is growing more complex each year. All together that adds up to pin graphics:

 ▪ Management sciences for coping with the complexities of such factors as personnel management, production technique, and the economics of practice.

 ▪ Computer advancements that occur so rapidly that thorough study of system capabilities is necessary to avoid quick obsolescence.

To get the most from pin graphics, the architect starts with overlays so the eventual transition to CAD will be accomplished without the danger of being not well enough prepared for a new, strange, difficult, and expensive way of producing drawings.

Nobody knows architectural production as the architect does, and therein may lie the reason for slow advances in drafting room progress. Computer promoters may know computers and reprographic salesmen may know repro-graphics, but they cannot possibly know drafting room production. Architects tend to lean on professionals who may be experts in their field, but it is the architect who must become expert in those fields. The architect has to master drafting room production and then computers and reprographics and become an authority on pin graphics. Until that is an accepted fact, rapid advances in drafting room practice will not be possible.

Glossary

Acetate: Synthetic, transparent film similar to nitrate film but not as flammable. Used as the photographic base called safety film. Available with smooth or matte surface.

Aperture card: A card with rectangular hole or holes specifically prepared for mounting microfilm frames.

Archival quality: A term applied to processed prints or films that are highly resistant to deterioration during use and storage.

Autopositive: A direct-positive polyester film or photographic paper print made by exposure on a contact printer.

Azo dye: The dye that is the basis for the diazo reproduction processes; it is a chemical compound produced by the reaction of a diazonium compound with a coupler.

Background: The area of a print without images. It may contain shading.

Background drawing: A drawing that contains information provided by architects for engineers and others who develop supplemental data. Becomes a base sheet when punched for pin registration.

Base color: The tint of base stock during manufacture.

Base stock: Polyester film, paper, or other material to which a sensitized coating is applied.

Block out: To cover up blemishes and unwanted data on film with opaquing fluid, tape, ink, black paper, or orange paper.

Blowback: The projection of an image by a process camera-projector unit onto sensitized film or paper.

Blue line: A diazo print with a white background and blue line.

Blueprint: A negative image formed by white lines on a blue background produced by a wet process on iron-sensitized paper.

Brown-line print: A print with a brown image line on a white background produced on silver-sensitized paper by printing through a negative.

Brownprint: A print made on material coated with light-sensitive iron and silver salts, which produce a negative brown image line from a positive master. Also called a vandyke.

Camera, fixed, multiposition: See *fixed multiposition camera.*

Camera, planetary: See *planetary camera.*

Camera, rotary: See *rotary camera.*

Camera, step and repeat: See *step-and-repeat camera.*

Card image: The microfilm frame of an aperture card or the exposed and processed output of a mounter, card-to-card printer, or roll-to-card printer.

Color transparency: A film positive, usually on an acetate base and in colors, to be viewed by transmitted light as by a projector.

COM: Abbreviation for computer output microfilm, which is produced by a recorder from computer-generated electrically powered signals.

Composite: The product of printing a series of base sheets and overlays by pin registration onto silver-sensitized polyester film, diazo film, or diazo paper by either contact printing or process camera-projector multiple-negative projection.

Contact frame: Reprographics equipment for making prints. Usually it has a vacuum arrangement for keeping originals and sensitized sheet material in close contact with each other.

Contact print: A photographic print produced by the exposure of an original on a sheet of photo- or diazo-sensitized material of the same size.

Continuous-tone copy: A photographic or diazo-printed image with gradations of tone as opposed to *line image,* which has no gradation of line strength.

Copyboard: A framed panel of glass for holding material to be photographed in either a horizontal or vertical position. Vertical copyboards are often front- and backlighted and equipped with powered vacuum to hold material flat and secure on the frame.

Copy negative: Processed film with a line image used to make an intermediate from which prints can be made.

Densitometer: An instrument for measuring the amount of incident light reflected or transmitted and thereby the optical density of an image.

Density: Relative darkness of an image.

Develop: To convert an invisible latent image to a visible image by use of a chemical solution.

Diazo: Short for the light-sensitive diazonium compound coating on either paper or polyester film that, after exposure to light and development by ammonia vapor, produces a line image.

Diazo vellum: A translucent paper sensitized with diazo compounds that produce black or sepia images.

Dimensional stability: The capacity of film or paper to retain original size and shape while being processed and in aging.

Direct positive: An image produced on film or paper without a negative by means of a positive-to-positive type of silver emulsion.

Drawdown: The action produced by vacuum in a flatbed printing frame to get flat, tight contact between the original and the paper or film reproduction material.

Drawing: An image produced either manually or by computer on paper, vellum, linen, or matte-surface polyester film.

Dropout: Portions of an original that, usually by accident, do not appear on a reproduction.

Dummy: A sketch used to guide the layout of a job for printing.

Electrostatic process: A reproduction process in which images are produced by electric charges induced by artificial light.

Emulsion: A coating of light-sensitive chemicals on paper or polyester film that, when exposed to light, takes a latent image that can be made visible by chemical processing.

Enlarge: To produce, by optical projection, a print larger than the original.

Enlarger: Photographic equipment for making enlarged prints.

Eradicator: A chemical solution for removing line images from a particular kind of sensitized sheet material.

Exposure: The predetermined interval for the introduction of light at a selected intensity to light-sensitive emulsions.

Facsimile: A process for scanning fixed images and transmitting them electronically to produce exact copies of the originals.

Fading: Loss of image density.

Film: A polyester or acetate base material with a draftable matte surface that is coated with a light-sensitive photographic or diazo emulsion.

Film holder: A device in which a film negative is mounted inside a camera or a process camera-projector. It may have pins for registration.

Film positive: A positive image on a photographic film.

Film speed: The characteristic of an emulsion that has to do with the degree of sensitivity. In the ASA number system, the higher the number the more sensitive the film.

Finishing: The final procedure of retouching, spotting, and coloring photographic products.

Fixed line: A line image that can be erased only with a two-part chemical solution.

Fixed multiposition camera: A camera with a fully adjustable negative and copyboard capability. It is available in low-bed and overhead-rail design.

Fixing: The process of removing unexposed silver salts from film emulsion to prevent any further reaction of the emulsion to light.

Foil plate: The sensitized plate used for offset printing. It is exposed through an intermediate negative to high-intensity light and then developed to produce a positive image ready for the press.

Format: The area of artwork for layout of drawings and pasteups.

Frame: A section of film containing an individual microfilm or motion picture.

Gelatin: The basic substance of a photographic emulsion in which light-sensitive salts are in suspension.

Generation: The consecutive stages of reproduction from an original.

Ghost: An unwanted image, usually an incomplete erasure appearing on a reproduction.

Halftone: A photographic reproduction in which gradations of tone are produced by variously spaced dots formed by a screen interposed between camera lens and film. Quality is determined by the fineness of the screen.

Horizontal enlarger: Equipment that projects onto a horizontal rather than vertical surface. It is used for making large photographic prints and murals, although newer camera-projector units with large vertical copyboards have the same capability.

Image: The appearance of the subject on a reproduction.

Intermediate: A reproduction of an original produced on translucent or transparent sheet material. It is used in place of the more expensive original for printing purposes.

Internegative: A negative used as an intermediate stage for photographic reproduction.

Interpositive: A positive used as an intermediate stage for photographic reproduction.

Itek: An offset printing system using a paper plate and an Itek camera.

Keynoting: The combining of numbers and notes usually as a time-saving measure. The notes are typed and keyed by numbers to various parts of a drawing.

Line copy: Generally black-and-white originals with only lines and solids and no intermediate tones.

Line negative: A high-contrast negative used in reproductions and not needing intermediate tones.

Lithography: Printing from one of a variety of surfaces on which the image is ink-receptive and the background or blank area is ink-repellent. See also *offset printing*.

Make ready: To prepare for lithographic printing.

Mask: To use opaque paper or cardboard to prevent certain areas of an original or negative from appearing on a reproduction.

Master: The original matter, such as a drawing or pasteup, from which reproductions are made.

Matte surface: The factory-applied drafting surface of a polyester film; it has a "tooth" for accepting pencil or ink.

Microfiche: A group of micro images on one piece of photographic film.

Microfilm: A greatly reduced photographic image for miniaturized storage of data.

Mode: The designation of a particular variety of imaging material; for example, "positive mode" indicates positive-acting material.

Moist-erasable film: A polyester sheet from which a reproduction image can be removed with a moistened eraser.

Mount: To position a drawing or print on heavy cardboard, board, or other rigid sheet material for display or protection purposes.

Multiple exposure: More than one exposure onto the same sheet of light-sensitive material.

Mural: A photographic reproduction in very large size.

Negative: A copy of an original in which the dark and light areas are reversed.

Nonreproducible: That which will not photograph, usually blue lines that are not to be printed.

Offset: A printing method that most commonly uses photographic negatives to transfer images to light-sensitive thin plates for mounting on presses. The inked image is transferred to a rubber blanket that, in turn, offsets the image onto a sheet of paper. See also *lithography*.

Opacity: The degree to which material will not transmit light. The quality is valuable when dark objects are on or in contact with the back of a sheet.

Opaque copy: Copy that must be reproduced by reflected light because it does not transmit light.

Orthochromatic: Photographic material that is sensitive to ultraviolet light and all colors except red, which reproduces as black does.

Overlay: A sheet containing hand-drawn or computer-generated data. It is prepunched for pin registration so it can be worked on separately from basic data.

Panchromatic: Photographic material that is sensitive to ultraviolet light and to all colors of the visible spectrum, which reproduce in approximately equivalent shades of gray.

Pasteup: An assembly of graphic materials produced by pasting or taping the materials to a sheet of film or paper.

Photodrafting: A way to put photos on sheet material for further drafting work or as reference data for use during completion of a drawing. Often regarded as a general term for most reprographics.

Photogrammetry: A photographic technique for making maps.

Photomechanical process: The means of producing copies by photography and chemical reaction.

Photomural: Wall-size enlargement of a photograph.

Photopolymer: Chemical compounds that react to light.

Photostat: Usually a right-reading, low-cost paper copy; a positive reproduction with black line image.

Pin bar: A narrow strip of thin metal with a standard number of small round pins uniformly spaced along it. Also called a registration bar.

Planetary camera: A camera for making microfilms. The documents being photographed and the film remain stationary during exposure.

Plate: A metal, paper, or plastic sheet that has an ink-receptive image and is used in lithographic and offset printing.

Plotter: A drafting device for producing lines by electronic means, usually a computer. In photogrammetry, a device used to create contour maps.

Point light source: A high-intensity electric light capable of producing greater sharpness than broad source lamps including those arranged in a bank. It requires the use of a high-quality lens.

Polyester film: A sheet material that has outstanding characteristics, high strength, dimensional stability, and long life.

Positive: A photographic or diazo reproduction with the same appearance as an original.

Print-back: A direct-reading copy made from a reverse-reading intermediate.

Printed circuit: An electric circuit produced on appropriate sheet material from artwork by photography, etching, or silk screening.

Process: A series of treatment steps such as developing, fixing, washing, and drying to produce a visible, permanent image. Wash-off processing provides an erasable image on film, photo, and diazo.

Process camera-projector: A photographic device capable of making reduced-size negatives and also projecting the negatives to make same-size, enlarged, or reduced positives.

Projection image: Photographic image achieved through a lens and enlarged, reduced, or made same size.

Projection print: A photographic print with an image produced through a lens: either enlarged, same size, or reduced.

Pulsed xenon lamp: A vacuum frame lamp with high and constant color temperature and a spectral output similar to that of sunlight.

Reader: A device for viewing small-negative, microfilm images.

Reader-printer: A reader with the capability of producing a copy of the microfilm image being viewed.

Reflex printer: Photographic equipment for producing same-size positive prints from opaque instead of translucent originals.

Registration: Precision alignment of images on different sheets superimposed on either the drafting board or a copyboard.

Registration bar: A narrow strip of thin metal with a number of small round pins uniformly spaced along it. Also called a pin bar.

Reproducible: A photo or diazo reproduction on film or translucent vellum that can be used to make other reproducible prints or whiteprints. Often used to save wear and tear on the original. One of a number of terms with essentially the same meaning; the others are second original, intermediate, and transparency.

Resolution: A measure of the sharpness of a reproduced image expressed as the number of visible lines per millimeter.

Restoration: A process of improving damaged worn originals by opaquing, masking, and photographic technique.

Reverse: Printing in which data appear as white on black.

Reverse-read print: A reproduction in which the image is right-reading from the front side of the sheet but is on the back side of the sheet.

Right reading: Letters and images that read properly because they appear in the same manner on the reproduction as on the original.

Roll-to-roll printer: Photographic equipment that produces duplicates of microfilm frames by contact printing.

Rotary camera: A camera for making microfilms. Documents are photographed while held in place and moved on a transport system that connects films and documents together during the photographic procedure.

Scale: The ratio of an image to actual size. Also, the range of gray densities in a specified range of exposures.

Scaling: Selecting a portion of a photograph to be reproduced in a certain new size.

Scissors drafting: Cutting out unwanted detail to either eliminate it or provide space for new data.

Screen: A sheet containing a pattern of lines or dots and spaces used to reduce the blackness of a photo image as in making a print with the background data subdued.

Scribe film: A polyester film with a thin, opaque coating that can be cut or removed with a stylus without damaging the base.

Second original: See *reproducible.*

Sensitized material: Sheet material coated with an emulsion containing a chemical that is sensitive to light.

Separation negatives: Negatives used for color printing. They are produced with filters and have densities that are appropriate to the primary colors used.

Sepia: A brown-line diazo product that is opaque to ultraviolet light. An alternative to black line.

Shadow print: A subdued image. Same as screened print.

Shelf life: A measure of resistance to deterioration during storage.

Silk screen process: A method of printing carried out by passing a pigmented substance through a stencil made of silk or other fine screening.

Silver film: A photographic film coated with an emulsion that contains silver halide.

Silver halide: A light-sensitive compound of silver and a halogen (fluorine, chlorine, bromine, or iodine).

Slick: A polyester film without a draftable matte surface. One side of the film may be coated with a light-sensitive emulsion. A totally clear film can be used for appliqué drafting with press-on materials.

Sodium thiosulfate: The primary chemical in a photo fixing bath. Ammonium thiosulfate also is used for fixing.

Spectral sensitivity: A rating of the sensitivity of an emulsion to electromagnetic waves.

Stabilization: A photographic fixing method in which the remaining silver halides are converted to stable compounds instead of removed.

Static: Friction-created electric charge that is particularly troublesome when the humidity is below 40%. Light from static can make marks on film or photo paper.

Step-and-repeat camera: A camera, used for making microfilms, that photographs a series of documents in predetermined orderly rows and columns on an area of film.

Still development: Film development with agitation during only the first 15 sec in order to produce fine lines.

Stop bath: A chemical rinse for stopping development.

Stripping: Aligning negatives. Also, cutting and placing a negative in a mask in preparation for final production.

Sulfurized image: Brown stain on film caused by improper fixing.

Tint: A dot pattern that reproduces as one tone. Also, a screen that results in a subdued image.

Tint screen: A screen formed of equal-size dots instead of solid lines.

Tooth: A characteristic of the matte surface applied to a sheet of material for drafting purposes.

Transillumination: Back lighting of a copyboard; light shines through the mounted copy instead of being reflected from it.

Translucent: Partially transparent.

Transmission: Passage of light through a material as during the production of intermediates and transparent negatives.

Transparency: A color positive that is viewed by transmitted light as in a slide projector.

Transparentizing: Treating the paper base of an intermediate to make it more translucent and increase printing speed.

Tungsten-quartz lamp: A light used in small vacuum frames for contact printing and for copyboard illumination.

Vacuum back: A suction device for holding film in a process camera.

Vacuum board: A copyboard on which copy is held in place by vacuum.

Vacuum frame: A type of flatbed printing equipment that uses a vacuum to hold originals and emulsion-coated sheets together in flat, smooth, positive contact.

Vandyke: See *brownprint.*

Vellum: A paper product that has been chemically treated to make it translucent for use as an original tracing in either pencil or ink.

Vertical copy camera: A photographic device in which the copyboard is horizontal and either the camera or the copyboard travels vertically.

Wash-off film: A photographic film with a light-sensitive emulsion that produces an image that can be erased with a moistened eraser.

Xerography: A method of copying and duplicating by use of electrostatic charges. It produces positive-to-positive opaque printing.

Index

General Services Administration (GSA), 101
Generation, definition of, 172
Ghost, 62, 172
Government and regulatory agencies, benefits
    of overlay system to, 150, 157
Grading plan drawing for land development
    project, 96
Graphics, building, overlay system applied to,
    89, 90
Green, Edward J., 36
Grid, framing (see Framing grid)

Halftone, definition of, 172
Hand drafting, traditional, 40–41
Heating systems, overlays for, 144–145
Horizontal enlarger, definition of, 172

Image, definition of, 172
Innovation, resistance to, 8
Intermediates, 103, 172
Intermittent method of production, 110
Internegative, definition of, 172
Interpositive, definition of, 172
Itek, definition of, 172

Keynoting, definition of, 172
Kitchens, overlay system for design of, 127

Land development, overlay system applied to,
    91–97
    base sheets, 92–94
    composites, 96–97
    design categories for overlays, 94–96
    existing topo survey, 94
    grading plan drawing, 96
    landscape plan, 96
    layout plan, development of, 93
    materials and tools, 92, 94
    overlay preparation, 94–97
    paving plan overlay, 96
    phasing and demolition drawings, 96
    placing buildings, 93–94
    plant layout drawings, 96
    production techniques, 92–94
    recreating facilities drawing, 96
    site structure drawing, 96
    site utilities drawing, 95–96
    soil-boring data, 94
    soil erosion drawing, 95
Landscape plan for land development project,
    96

Layout (see Base sheet)
Legends and symbols overlay for electrical de-
    sign, 147
Lighting layout in ceiling design, 118–119
Lighting overlays, 147, 148
Line copy, definition of, 172
Line negative, definition of, 172
Lithography, definition of, 172
Logical sequencing, 34

McGregor, Douglas, 11
Make ready, definition of, 172
Management:
    administrative technique in, 32
    communicating in, 36–37
    coordinating in, 35–36
    directing in, 37
    expert, value of, 8–10
    organizing in, 33
    planning in, 32
    principles of, 31–32
    scheduling in, 33–35
Management science, pioneers of, 10
Management tools, 39–47
    forms control, 39–40
    and planning work, 46–47
    problem solving, 40
    project manual, 41–46
    and schematics and design development, 46
    systems, 40–41
Mask, definition of, 172
Master, definition of, 172
Master control index, 35, 70
Matte surface, definition of, 172
Mechanization of drafting room, 1–8
Medical facilities, overlay system for design of,
    127
Microfiche, definition of, 172
Microfilm, definition of, 172
Mini-plan, 42
Mode, definition of, 172
Moist-erasable film, 52, 173
Mount, definition of, 173
Multicolored drawings, reasons for using, 8
Multiple exposure, definition of, 173
Multiple-negative projection, 60, 62, 64
Mural, definition of, 173

Negative, definition of, 173
Negative engraving, 13–15
Nonreproducible, definition of, 173
Notes overlay, 114–116, 141–142
Numbering system, overlay-register, 69–71

Offset, definition of, 173

About the Author

C. W. *Edwards* has been employed for fifteen years with the architectural firm of Faulkner, Fryer and Vanderpool in Washington, DC. He has spent years studying new developments in better drafting room production of drawings for construction projects, including photos, stickyback materials, appliqué materials, paste-up, scissors, and finally overlay drafting. He also spent a year studying reproduction technology in one of the largest facilities in the east and made some of the first presentations on overlay and management to architects, universities, and reprographic associations.